Americanizing Japanese Firms

The Institutionalization of Corporate Philanthropy and Volunteerism in American Communities

Yukio Yotsumoto

UNIVERSITY PRESS OF AMERICA,® INC.

Lanham • Boulder • New York • Toronto • Plymouth, UK

Copyright © 2010 by
University Press of America,® Inc.
4501 Forbes Boulevard
Suite 200
Lanham, Maryland 20706
UPA Acquisitions Department (301) 459-3366

Estover Road
Plymouth PL6 7PY
United Kingdom

Library of Congress Control Number: 2009941767
ISBN: 978-0-7618-4988-9 (paperback : alk. paper)
eISBN: 978-0-7618-4989-6

Contents

Illustrations

Acknowledgments

This publication was supported by Ritsumeikan Asia Pacific University Academic Publication Support Program.

The manuscript was written based on nine years of my study. For this manuscript, I revised my dissertation titled "Corporate Social Responsibility (CSR) of Japanese Manufacturing Companies in a Kentucky Community: A Case Study", submitted to the University of Kentucky in December 2002, and in papers published in the journals below:

"Firm Size and Corporate Giving: An Exploratory Study of Japanese and American Manufacturing Firms in an American Rural Community." *Keiei to Seido (Journal of Business and Institutions),* No. 3, Pp. 1–18, 2005. (In corroboration with Nobuhide Hatasa).

"An Examination of Corporate Participation in Civil Society: A Case Study on Japanese firms in Kentucky, U.S.A." *Ritsumeikan Bungaku (The Journal of Cultural Sciences-The Ritsumeikan Bungaku),* No. 591, Pp. 251–264, 2005. (Written in Japanese).

"Corporate Attitudes toward Philanthropy among Japanese, American and British Manufacturing Firms in a Kentucky Community." *Keiei to Seido (Journal of Business and Institutions),* No. 4, Pp. 13–29, 2006. (In corroboration with Nobuhide Hatasa).

I would like to acknowledge my appreciation to Professor Pradyumna P. Karan (University of Kentucky), Professor Lorraine Garkovich (University of Kentucky), Professor Yuji Yamamoto (Osaka International University), Professor Nobukiyo Eguchi (Ritsumeikan University) and Professor Masami Fujimaki (Ritsumeikan University) for their encouragement in my academic career.

Chapter One

Introduction

As globalization progresses, the outward investment of Japanese multinational corporations has increased worldwide. The United States has been the number one market for Japanese firms[1] and after the Plaza Accord in September 22, 1985, in which the depreciation of the U.S. dollar to the Japanese yen and German Deutsche Mark was agreed upon, Japanese firms partly shifted their corporate strategy from export to foreign direct investment in order to reduce the loss caused by the appreciation of the Japanese yen. This trend will continue as the world becomes increasingly borderless. For example, Japan's outward foreign direct investment increased from 258,653 million dollars in December 1996 to 449,680 million dollars in December 2006. When we look at Japan's foreign direct investment to the United States, it also shows an increase from 97,881 million dollars in December 1996 to 156,411 million dollars in December 2006 (Japan External Trade Organization 2008a).

Foreign direct investment is not just capital movement, but involves social and cultural encounters of different societies. When Japanese firms build factories and do business in America, they meet various challenges associated with social and cultural differences. This is felt even more keenly when they interact with communities where they build factories. Community has norms and expectations that are formed by its history, citizens and social trends. So, Japanese people need to learn the cultures of local communities. Also, when Japanese firms interact with communities in America, they have to gain an understanding of the norms and expectations in order to successfully establish a business. On the side of local citizens who receive Japanese expatriates, it is also true that they have to learn the way Japanese think and behave in order to have positive interactions with Japanese.

An interesting local trend can be found in Lexington, Kentucky where there has been an influx of Japanese people for the past ten years. More Japanese

1

are seen shopping in malls and Japanese children attending American schools. A Japanese Saturday school has also emerged, operating out of a local middle school. Likewise, more Japanese restaurants are now available in town than before, with five now in business in Lexington alone. Even in some small rural counties of Kentucky,[2] local residents now have more opportunities to associate and interact with Japanese people and learn their culture. Often this is their first opportunity to meet people from another country. Now, citizens in rural Kentucky communities can feel the atmosphere of an international community.

These changes took place because Kentucky has received a large amount of direct investment from Japan. In 1999, the total investment to Kentucky reached 6.9 billion dollars (Karan, 2001). Since the 1980s, Japanese manufacturing companies have been establishing their facilities in Kentucky, which grew to 137 companies operating in the state by 2004 (Kentucky Cabinet for the Economic Development, 2004). The state of Kentucky is a winner in the smokestack chase, a battle among communities, states and nations to attract factories. Economically, investments by Japanese corporations in Kentucky have generated numerous jobs and tax revenues for the state. For example, there are more than 35,000 Kentuckians employed by Japanese companies (Kentucky Cabinet for the Economic Development, 2002). It also created a ripple effect for new jobs. Toyota, for example, brought many subsidiary companies when it built a large factory. Also, the employees' consumption in localities generated many retail store jobs.

Although we see more Japanese corporations in Kentucky communities, socially, the impact on those communities is not well known, given the near absence of sociological studies on the issue. Thus, for one thing, this study is a contribution to fill the gap. In other words, this study is designed to understand the social implications of the presence of Japanese corporations on the surrounding Kentucky communities. This study also provides a cross-cultural perspective in understanding corporate social responsibility in American communities. It specifically examines the phenomenon as a factor in host community responses to the entry of new foreign economic enterprises. This topic, too, has not been explored well in sociology and community development studies, thus, this research tries to contribute to those areas.

THE PRESENT STUDY

This study examines the concept of corporate social responsibility in Japanese manufacturing companies in Kentucky. The concept of corporate social responsibility was chosen because it deals with the intersection of business and community/society. Besides providing jobs and taxes, businesses can engage in communities through corporate philanthropy. This is one of the interesting social phenomena in which interactions between business and community can be observed. It is a useful concept to begin exploring the social impacts of Japanese manufacturing companies on Kentucky communities.

This is an exploratory study which compares Japanese companies with American companies and a British company in regard to corporate philanthropy. Also, Japanese companies are compared among themselves regarding corporate philanthropy. First, an investigation of how the characteristics of Japanese manufacturing companies influence their level and nature of corporate philanthropy is undertaken. Second, a relationship between the size and the level & nature of corporate social responsibility is examined. Finally, how Japanese corporations learn about the American approach of corporate philanthropy is explored. When investigating the above research questions, I considered two contexts in which activities of corporate social responsibility are carried out. The first context is the societies of Japan and the United States at national level. The constitutions of each society are analyzed so that we can understand the position or importance of corporate philanthropy within the societies comparatively. The second context is the community under investigation, in which corporations are located and act for social contribution. A community is a dynamic place where social interactions take place.[3] Wilkinson (1991) shows the dynamic aspects of a community in which residents and local organizations have the capacity to overcome structural constrains in order to develop their community. He tries to conceptualize 'community' as a social interaction that has the three elements of a locality, a local society and a community field. A locality means a territory where people live and meet their daily needs together. A local society is a comprehensive network of associations for meeting common needs and expressing common interests. A community field is a process of interrelated actions through which residents and local organizations express their common interest in the local society. In his theory, community actions are the manifestation of the community field. Here, the dynamic and emergent aspects of community life are emphasized, allowing community development to occur. Thus, activities of corporate philanthropy, as a manifestation of social interaction, can be understood more fully by examining the web of community interaction.

OUTLINE OF CHAPTERS

This study consists of nine chapters. Chapter two is a review of literature: it is an overview of studies relevant to corporate social responsibility. The first section is a summary of sociological approaches to corporate social responsibility. These studies help us to understand how the idea of corporate social responsibility has emerged. Researchers in this area investigate the social origin of corporate social responsibility and critically evaluate its function in society. It also clarifies what kind of social interactions have been formed in this phenomenon. Norm and/or networks in corporate social responsibility are important concepts for the analysis. The second section is a discussion of business and management approaches to corporate social responsibility, an academic field where the majority of research on corporate social responsibility has been conducted. Since there are a great number of studies, I focused on two key study areas: studies on the acceptance or rejection of corporate social responsibility and studies about defining and conceptualizing corporate social responsibility. The third section is a summary of comparative approaches to corporate social responsibility. Mainly, the discussion is focused on Japanese corporate social responsibility in comparison to that in the United States. The final section of this chapter is a discussion of institutional theory in organizational literature. This section is included because institutional theory is thought to be helpful in analyzing this social phenomenon. It provides a keen standpoint to see the process and factors for institutionalizing corporate social responsibility within firms and society.

Chapter three is a section on sociological methods. It starts with a discussion of the method used in this study. Since a case study was selected as a method for investigation, the strengths and weaknesses of case study methods are discussed. Next, steps to arrive at selecting the city of Heartland as this research site are reported. Then definition and operationalization of key concepts in this study are introduced. This section will help a reader to understand the discussion in the following chapters. Data collection and data analysis are the next discussion. Interview procedures and researcher's personal experiences while contacting people are mentioned. Because qualitative research has an emergent process, the data analysis section is brief and general. In the final part of the chapter, the limitations of this research in terms of design and data collection are mentioned. This will help readers to design future research on this topic.

Chapter four is a discussion of the community where the corporations are studied. Although this is a discussion of a context, it is a very important section in this study. This is because one of the research interests is the interaction between business and community/society. Without contextualizing the issue, researchers may end up with superficial findings. Also, in organization theories, environment is a key concept in understanding organizational behaviors. In the first part of this chapter, socio-economic profiles of the city with historical trends are described. In the second part, Kentucky Bluegrass United Way is described. Because this organization is a key actor in philanthropic activities in Heartland, it helps us to understand the expectation of the community and what kinds of activity are available in the community.

Chapter five is a discussion of human resource management and its effect on the level and nature of corporate social responsibility. It describes how companies view the concept of corporate social responsibility and what they actually do in philanthropy. In discussing this issue, the focus is on the relationship between corporate giving and recruitment & retention of workers. This relationship reveals that American, Japanese and British firms conceive the functional meaning of corporate social responsibility in human resource management differently.

Chapter six looks at firm size and its effects on corporate giving. Size and its impacts on corporate structure and behavior are one of the most researched areas in organizational studies as well as studies on corporate social responsibility. What sets this research apart from the rest of existing literature is that it is a qualitative one and focuses on Japanese companies in the United States. In understanding the behavior of Japanese firms on corporate giving, the idea of institutionalization was found to be very helpful.

In chapter seven, I look at the differences in the constitution of society between Japan and the United States. Corporate philanthropy is situated in the discussion of civil society, the business sector and the government so that we can understand more clearly why the difference in the conception of corporate philanthropy exists between Japanese and Americans.

Chapter eight focuses on how Japanese corporations learn about corporate giving in the United States. Corporate social responsibility is an idea unique to American society. Therefore, Japanese corporations must learn how to practice corporate giving. Three ways of learning corporate philanthropy are identified. They are learning from the literature, learning from employees, and learning from the community. This chapter also compares American and Japanese companies to clarify the underlying difference between Japanese and American views on corporate giving. It helps to explain why Japanese firms need to learn the culture of corporate philanthropy in America.

The final chapter is a conclusion of this study. In the first part, the findings are summarized. Then, the implications of this research are discussed. This is a discussion of application. Suggestions are made for both donors (Japanese corporations) and recipients (non-profit organizations) for better philanthropy. Finally, several suggestions for future research will be mentioned.

NOTES

1. Between 1990 and 2007, the United States was the number one market for Japan. However, its share declined from 31.5 percent in 1990 to 20.1 in 2007. This is due to the rise of China as a Japanese business partner. China became the number two

market for Japan, with a share of 15.3 percent in 2007. It was the 12th market for Japan with a share of 2.1 percent in 1990 (Japan External Trade Organization 2008b).

2. Here, it should be noted that not all rural Kentucky communities receive Japanese foreign direct investment. As many of the companies that establish facilities are related to auto industries, they tend to locate factories near the Interstate highways of 75, 65 and 64, so that they can deliver products in the Just-in-Time management system. Therefore, they do not have much investment in the eastern part of Kentucky (Appalachian Mountain area), which is geographically isolated and considered to be one of the poorest regions of America.

3. There are many theories on community, ranging from a structural-functional perspective to the perspective of symbolic interactionism. This study adopts Wilkinson's conception of community, because it describes the dynamic nature of community by emphasizing agency.

Chapter Two

Literature Review

INTRODUCTION

Corporate citizenship and corporate social responsibility have been identified by business and government circles, as well as citizens, as approaches to solving social problems. Governments in many countries try to balance their budgets and reduce the responsibilities of government. Therefore, they look to alternative actors who can take on some of the responsibility for solving social predicaments. On the side of business, participation in social contribution is appealing because it enhances their positive image in society. It is a part of their branding strategy. While a large body of literature exists in this area, most has been conducted by scholars in business/management fields. It is natural to see the publication from those scholars since corporate social responsibility is a function of businesses and research from the field has provided direct implications for better management.

The areas of interest in corporate social responsibility from the business/management field are how to define and measure corporate citizenship and corporate social responsibility as well as to identify strategies for effective programs of corporate social responsibility. In business, the idea of corporate social responsibility emerged in the 1970s and gained momentum after the 1980s. As the idea was new at that time, it was of critical importance to understand exactly what it was. Also, as the activity costs money to corporations, finding and recommending cost-effective measures of corporate citizenship activities were important tasks for scholars in business and management.

Gradually, corporate social responsibility and corporate citizenship as concepts and practices have gained the interest of both academics and business leaders. However, not many scholarly studies have focused on the broader social contexts surrounding these concepts.

In this literature review section, the first three subsections deal with various studies directly related to corporate social responsibility. The first subsection is a review of sociological approaches to corporate social responsibility. Sociological approaches to corporate social responsibility are minor compared to business and management approaches; however, they provide us with a very unique angle of understanding. The uniqueness comes from the disciplinary tradition that focuses community and society at large. The second subsection is a summary of business and management approaches to corporate social responsibility. The majority of studies on corporate social responsibility are conducted from the business and management perspectives. There are a great number of articles and books on the topic. In order to present the issue succinctly, I focus two areas of study, namely, studies that discuss whether corporate social responsibility is necessary or not, and studies that try to capture its essence. The third subsection looks at corporate social responsibility from Japanese perspectives. This subsection provides us with important background information for the discussion that follows in this manuscript. The final subsection reviews institutional theories in organizational literatures. Studies by Himmelstein (1996), Galaskiewicz (1991) and Besser (1998) which will be reviewed shortly indicate the importance of norms and networks in a community for better performance of corporate social responsibility. Also, Bob (1990) and Taka (1997) reviewed below show the influence of cultural factors on corporate citizenship. These studies lead us to the studies of norms and adaptation. Institutional theories have generated a rich volume of work on these issues. Therefore, the final subsection is a review of institutional theories in general and their implications for this research.

SOCIOLOGICAL APPROACHES TO CORPORATE SOCIAL RESPONSIBILITY

Although studies on corporate social responsibility from sociology are not as many as studies from business and management, they provide us with unique perspectives on the subject, such as its origin, its relationship with culture, and interactional aspects within and outside of it.

A broad and critical argument on corporate social responsibility was made by Jones (1996), who used a political economy paradigm to criticize the concept of corporate social responsibility, concluding that this is not a sustainable strategy and scholars are too naive on the issue. The political economy paradigm is a critique of capitalist political economy. It tries to reveal structural mechanisms that protect and foster capitalism and to find contradictions that may cause its failure. It is a Marxian approach which sees a contradiction in the dialectic of thesis, antithesis and synthesis and which sees capitalism as a system that will eventually fail.

Jones contends that the concept of corporate social responsibility is an ideology that legitimizes the capitalist political economy, by maintaining the status quo of capitalism. He traces the historical origin of corporate social responsibility to the seminal work of Berle and Means, published in 1932. They studied the separation of ownership and control in business, which became an influential paradigm called managerialism in business and organizational research. Berle and Means argue that professional managers become stewards of society's resources because they are the group that can manage resources most efficiently for society. This is the beginning of the idea of corporate social responsibility. As a direct successor of managerialism, Jones sees corporate social responsibility as unsustainable, because the emergence of institutional shareholders, program trading and a market for corporate control in the 1980s undermined professional managers' powers as stewards for society.

Recently, the process has accelerated and we see the growing power of shareholders in corporations relative to managers and employees, which is observed in many countries. It was reinforced mainly by three changes in society. First, the recent technological innovations in information technology, such as computers, made it possible to transact money instantly. Second, the development of new money products allowed more volume and flexibility in investment. Third, the increasing influence of neo-liberal ideas supported by organizations such as the World Trade Organization permeates the globe. More recently, in the case of Japan, there has been an increase of news coverage in which Japanese managers are pressured to accept proposals made by foreign investors.

Another critique of corporate social responsibility is based on manager's behavior, which Jones contends is derived from profit-maximizing rather than socially responsible behavior. This tendency, he asserts, will increase as financial capital gains more power. Sometimes, managers are asked to meet the expectation of shareholders who tend to seek a short-term profit driven by self-interests. Jones' critical approach paints corporate social responsibility as an ideology that protects and fosters a capitalist economy which is moving towards failure, due to the growing power of shareholders.

Himmelstein (1996) is another scholar who contextualizes corporate philanthropy. He places it within a culture created by the interactions of corporate giving officers and networks of chief executive officers in community. Many corporations have corporate giving officers who come to share similar ideas about corporate giving. These officers attend professional meetings on philanthropy where they learn issues and strategies for effective programs. This is a structured setting for forming a common culture of corporate giving. Informally, corporate giving officers have peers in other companies with whom they share information about grants and nonprofit organizations, and ideas about where to donate. Corporate giving officers, as administrators of corporate giving, are socialized into the culture of corporate philanthropy through professionalization in which those administrators acquire integrity and competence in carrying out various corporate giving activities.

A network of chief executive officers and wealthy individuals is also an important factor in the formation of a culture of corporate giving. It is a normative aspect of corporate giving. By belonging to the network, they need to show they are leaders within the community, as it is expected among the members of the network and community. For example, the corporations have to be very active in charity to be prominent in the communities of Atlanta and Minneapolis (Chronicles of Philanthropy, 1994).

Galaskiewicz's study (1991) in Twin Cities, Minnesota, shows how an institution of corporate giving has been formed through the formalization of philanthropy, which makes philanthropy more sustainable. Companies contribute a certain percentage of their profits to charity, and this is a prerequisite for being perceived as a member of the local elite. In some communities, firms are expected to contribute 5 percent of their profits. The network of CEOs, therefore, creates a culture of charity which influences how much they should donate.

The institutionalization of corporate giving was carried out in three dimensions. First, public recognition was institutionalized. In Minneapolis-St. Paul, peer pressure among business elites motivated the firms' contribution to charity. However, as the elites grew older, the pressure for more contribution to charity became less effective. Instead of seeking the recognition of their peers, they built a mechanism in which donations to charity became recognized by the public. In this way, corporate giving was stabilized in a way that could no longer be affected by the changes of individual circumstances. Second, an ethic of enlightened self-interest was institutionalized. This ethic, in plain words, means: "What's good for society is good for our company" (Hay and Gray 1974: 140). It is a belief that a benefit is accrued by investing in community and society in a long-term perspective. Since the benefit cannot be measured tangibly, it has been criticized by some scholars. However, in Twin Cities, the establishment of a non-profit venture called the Minnesota Project on Corporate Responsibility (MPCR) in 1978 cleared a way for the ascendance of the ethic of enlightened self-interests. It has provided educational programs, held forums, acted as a catalyst to encourage cooperation among business, government and community organizations, and stimulated private sector initiative. Third, contributions were institutionalized within the company. At one time, all decisions on corporate giving were made by the chief executive officers and high ranking executives. However, formal contribution departments were established within the firm, where professional contributions officers work full-time or part-time. They are professionals who belong to professional associations and continuously polish their knowledge on philanthropy.

Himmelstein also contributes to the understanding of corporate philanthropy from a broad political framework, in which the position of corporate philanthropy in society is carefully circumscribed. In a prevailing understanding, nonprofit organizations are the independent sector, that is, independent from business and government. This is a term that describes the position of corporate philanthropy in American society. Drawing on Hall's (1982) argument, Himmelstein says that since the earliest days of the American Republic, elites, especially business elites, have distrusted the state and supported nonprofit organizations as an alternative to a government function of welfare. They envisioned that public goods should be delivered not by the government but by private hands. Although the emergence of social welfare programs since the New Deal undermined the reality of public service by private hands, the idea still survives as corporate philanthropy. The support for the independent sector serves as a form of protection from the encroachment of government into the private sector. Therefore, business' support for nonprofit organizations is not against the business' objective (profit making). An implication of this argument is that, for corporations, supporting nonprofit organizations is beneficial in the long term, because it functions as a form of protection for private enterprise. Another implication is that doing business means more than just short-term profit maximization. Corporations are also interested in prestige and honor that cannot be measured by short term profits, and participation in philanthropy brings just that.

Corporate social responsibility is an important factor for any community. When a community is declining, corporate social responsibility becomes an attractive concept for community development. Besser's research (1998) shows a connection between business social responsibility and community. Defining the concept, she uses three dimensions of business social responsibility developed by the Council of Economic Development (Post, 1996). The first dimension is a responsibility to consumers, employees and shareholders. A company is expected to produce cheap and safe products, to consider the welfare of its employees (i.e., are the employees' benefits good? Do they work in a safe workplace?), and to provide shareholders a reasonable return on their investment. The second dimension is a responsibility to the environment. Corporations, especially extractive and manufacturing industries, have degraded the environment in the past. Now, corporations are expected to be environmentally friendly. The third dimension is a responsibility to the community. This consists of contributions to the arts, solving social problems, and supporting community improvement programs. In her research, Besser focuses on the third dimension, a responsibility to the community. Though there are various studies on business social responsibility in relation to employees, shareholders, consumers and the employment, there are not many studies that investigate the relationship between business social responsibility and community directly. Thus, her study is an important contribution to this area.

Using data from 1,008 small business owners and managers in 30 Iowa communities, Besser tries to understand the impact of business operators' perceptions about the norms of collective action in their communities, as well as the level of their support for and commitment to their communities. Adopting quantitative methods, she analyzes their relationships within the community. She shows that business operators who feel that their communities have a higher level of norms of collective action are more likely to support their communities than business operators who feel that their communities have a lower level of collective action. As with Himmelstein and Galaskiewicz, this research shows how the importance of norms and networks within a community affects the degree of business social responsibility.

Besser's research is related to the concept of social capital, developed by Coleman (1982) and articulated by Putnam (1993). Social capital includes "features of social organization such as trust, norms, and networks, which can improve the efficiency of society by facilitating coordinated actions (Putnam, 1993)." Putnam was among the first to show the relationship between social capital and economic development, and Besser's research supports this relationship. To be successful in economic development, a community needs to nurture social capital. This concept entered into the mainstream of community development literature as it has good potential for explanation and application of community development. In this perspective, corporations are social organizations that are potential agents for development. The key factor for the transformation of potential agents to actual agents is whether or not community has nurtured trust, norms and networks for collective actions to develop the community.

From a different angle, Ostrander and Schervish (1990) try to understand philanthropy as a social relationship between donors and recipients whose actions are constrained by the larger societal context. This societal context can be analyzed using the idea of human agency and social structure. Human agency is human action that creates, maintains or changes social structure. Once social structure is created, it defines human actions by constraining or facilitating actions. In this structure, people are not passive actors. They can transform social structure through their actions. It is a process of creating and constraining between human agency and social structure. Using this idea, philanthropy can be seen as one form of social structure. Donors and recipients participate in this structure as agents who sustain or change it.

Ostrander and Schervish categorize patterns of philanthropy using donor and recipient relations. Philanthropy, a social structure, is constructed by two groups of actors, donors and recipients. They see mainly two types of social relations in philanthropy. One is a donor-oriented type; the other is recipient-oriented type. Currently, philanthropy is a donor-oriented world in which donors have determining power to shape the relationships. Donors have more power because the relationship is based on the transaction of morals or norms. This is much weaker than the relationship based on transactions of money or votes. Money or votes have more sanctioning or rewarding power than morals or norms. Therefore, in philanthropy, even if donors do not respond to recipients' needs, they may not feel many sanctions. When norms and morals are not backed by economic and political influence, they do not exert the power that alters donors' behaviors.

Ostrander and Schervish identify three major donor-side strategies which are based on different types of social relations. The first type is a personal-engagement strategy. Here, donors and recipients have direct personal contact and exchange information, and recipients' needs are highly considered. An example is consumption philanthropy where donors and recipients are the same. Donors contribute to churches, schools and cultural organizations, in which they are often members, therefore benefiting the donors also. The second type is a mediated-engagement strategy. In this type, donors and recipients do not have personal contact. Instead, they are mediated by a third party, such as grant seeking or advocacy organizations. Contributory philanthropy is an example. In this strategy, donations are solicited for a cause from people whom recipients have not met. Mail and phone solicitations are common methods for this strategy. Because of the mediating nature, donors do not receive the same type of direct benefits that donors involved in a personal-engagement strategy might. Rather, the benefit would be recognition from advocacy organizations and a sense of satisfaction they gain through altruistic action. Since it does not result in a direct and material benefit, it is generally a less encouraging strategy for motivating donation than the first type strategy. The third type is a donor-oriented strategy. In this type, recipients' needs are not so important, because donors contribute to a cause for their own purposes. An example is exchange philanthropy, where a firm contributes to a cause because of a request by friends of executives. They contribute to a cause hoping that this favor will be returned later by the person who asked. Therefore, in this type, partially, there is a rational aspect of calculating. It

also has a normative aspect in which tangible direct returns are not expected,
ᴀꜱ ɪɴ ᴛʜᴇ ᴄᴀꜱᴇ ᴏꜰ ꜰᴜʟʟy ᴅᴇᴠᴇʟᴏᴘᴇᴅ ʀᴀᴛɪᴏɴᴀʟ ᴀꜱᴘᴇᴄᴛ. ʜᴇʀᴇ, ᴛʜᴇ ɴᴏʀᴍ ʙᴇᴄᴏᴍᴇꜱ ᴀɴ
important factor in the decision over whether or not a donation will be made
and what amount. Galaskiewicz's study (1991) in Minneapolis-St. Paul, described above, depicts this type of social relation, in which the peer pressure
of business elites motivated a company's participation in philanthropy.

In recipient-side strategies, Ostrander and Schervish also describe three
major types of strategy which are based on different ways to frame needs:
needs-based, opportunity-based and agenda-based strategies, which are dif-
ferentiated by the recipient's degree of need. In a needs-based strategy that
places a higher emphasis on recipients' needs, this will become the basis of
solicitation, as opposed to the other two strategy types. Recipients frame a
cause as being worthy of the attention of donors. Solicitation from the United
Nations Children's Fund to improve children's nutrition or solicitation from
Doctors Without Borders to eradicate malaria are good examples of this type.
The shortcoming of this strategy type is that a cause framed by recipients'
needs may not attract attention from donors who are not conscious about
social issues.

In an opportunity-based strategy which expresses recipients' needs moder-
ately among the three, the needs of beneficiaries are framed as opportunities
for donors to obtain social and political benefits. For example, a contribution
to a community project may increase the status of the donor within the community. In this type, in order to attract donors, the needs which donors also
have an interest in are introduced.

Of the three recipient-side strategies, an agenda-based strategy will place
the lower priority on the needs of the beneficiary. Donors' needs are framed
as a program so that recipients can easily obtain donations from donors. However, although this strategy attracts the highest amount of donations, it can be
problematic due to its lack of recipient-needs focus, often creating programs
that are of no use to those they attempt to help.

By categorizing philanthropy in this way, Ostrander and Schervish try to
clarify the relationships between donors and recipients, and in doing so, show
that philanthropy is a donor oriented-world. Their study helps to transform
the social structure of philanthropy to one where recipients have more determining power. They offer a strategy, in which recipients can improve their
terms in the relationship, and they believe that by bringing recipients in, the
quality and performance of philanthropy will increase.

So far, several arguments on social responsibility by social scientists have
been summarized. Here, their works are briefly evaluated. Jones' political
economy approach starts from an assumption that capitalism and its ide-
ologizing concept, social responsibility, inherently and historically possesses

contradictions. In this case, the increased power of institutional shareholders who exhibit profit-maximizing behaviors on a short-term basis undermine the power of managers who seek the best use of resources for society. In recent years, globalization has accelerated this trend worldwide, and we see many incidences in which communities suffer job losses from plants closing, environmental degradation, deterioration of health care, etc. Thus, Jones' theory offers us a good analytic tool to understand recent social problems in communities, which are caused by the growing influence of institutional shareholders and program trading. However, profit-maximizing and socially responsible behaviors are not polarized concepts like Jones envisions. It is possible for a manager to pursue profit with socially responsible behavior. Or, alternatively it can be argued that long-term profit-maximizing implies socially responsible behavior. Probably, for firms' long-term survival, the integration of corporate social responsibility into their business strategies is necessary.

Both Jones and Himmelstein's discussions deal with the context in which corporate social responsibility and corporate philanthropy have emerged. They argue that culture is an important factor for how corporate social responsibility or corporate philanthropy has developed. Simply, Himmelstein describes how corporate philanthropy developed historically and how interactions among actors in philanthropy created its culture in the United States. On the other hand, Jones explicitly judges its existence using a Marxian approach, denying the sustainability of its idea and practice. Although both of them talk about the history of corporate philanthropy, Jones' discussion is limited to the early twentieth century, while Himmelstein traces back its origin to the earliest years of the American Republic. In contrast to Himmelstein's historical analysis, Jones' discussion is based more on the analysis of systems. Therefore, Jones perspective is more general and offers a broader understanding of the issue. It is especially helpful when we try to understand recent social problems, such as inequality caused by globalization.

Besser's research is a great contribution to corporate social responsibility research in sociology. In contrast to Himmelstein and Galaskiewicz's studies that are qualitative, Besser's study is quantitative, and the large sample (1,008) of interviews permits conclusions on more general terms. Also, the operationalization of the concept can expand the comparativeness of studies in this field. One shortcoming in her research is that it is based on self reports of business owners and managers. Therefore, a high level of business social responsibility in a community collected as data does not necessary means the community actually possesses a high level of business social responsibility. The subjective nature of the data makes it difficult to translate into objective interpretation. So, one approach to reduce the problem is to compare the community with other communities.

Ostrander and Schervish do not question philanthropy itself as much as Jones does. For them, it is given that philanthropy contributes to the betterment of society. Their view on philanthropy is closer to scholars in the business field. The difference is what constitutes philanthropy. Often, business scholars see philanthropy as a part of a business strategy recently expanded. Since it is a business strategy, their concerns are its effectiveness and efficiency within the overall business. On the other hand, in Ostrander and Schervish's view, philanthropy is a social relationship. Since it is a social relationship, both the business side and the recipient side are equally analyzed. Therefore, they have shown a different approach to philanthropy from business scholars.

BUSINESS/MANAGEMENT APPROACHES TO CORPORATE SOCIAL RESPONSIBILITY

There has been more research conducted on corporate social responsibility in the field of business than in the field of sociology. Business scholars have been interested in questions like: "what is corporate social responsibility?" and "how can we apply it to business?" In the beginning, the debate was whether business should embrace the idea of corporate social responsibility or be against it. As the social expectation of corporate social responsibility grew, it was gradually accepted by businesses. When the concept became defined as a component of the business function, discussions shifted from the issue of its legitimation to the best way to incorporate social responsibility into general business strategies.

Davis (1971) succinctly summarized the early debate of whether business should engage in social responsibility or not, listing several arguments for and against it. In his discussion, he defines corporate social responsibility as "the firm's consideration of, and response to, issues beyond the narrow economic, technical, and legal requirements of the firm." He further says that "it is the firm's obligation to evaluate in its decision-making process, the effects of its decisions on the external social system in a manner that will accomplish social benefits along with the traditional economic gains which the firm seeks. It means that social responsibility begins where the law ends (313)."

Major reasons for social responsibility are: long-run self-interest, public image, avoidance of government regulation, and socio-cultural norms. By improving the community where they do business, the company also receives long-term benefits. For example, when a company helps to improve local education, the company may expect to get a better quality labor force in the future. This will reduce the cost of training employees and increase productivity. Another example is that an improved community means a reduced crime rate. When the crime rate is low, it means less money for protecting property. Long-run self-interest, however, was difficult to measure, and the ambiguity over whether input could be matched by a desired and expected outcome was hardly a motivating factor in encouraging social responsibility. It also involves the free rider problem, and this receives severe resistance from the business sector. For example, ideally, a company's support for local education benefits the company in the form of high quality employees. However, the people who were educated through the support of the company may work for rival corporations that didn't contribute to the local education.

Corporations are conscious about creating a good public image. Companies have experienced sanctions from consumers and community residents when they received bad publicity from problems such as pollution and mismanagement. A good public image may bring more customers, better employees and other indirect benefits. It will increase a competitive advantage relative to other firms. In recent years, corporate social responsibility is strongly tied to branding strategies. A corporation's program in which planting a tree for reducing CO_2 is carried out when consumers purchase goods from them is a good example of a branding strategy.

Business also may want to be socially responsible in order to avoid government regulations, which can be costly and restrict corporation's decision making. Therefore, business acts for society before the government intervenes. This is especially true in the United States where the initiatives of the private sector were the foundation of nation building. This is an idea discussed in more detail by Himmelstein.

Socio-cultural norms also play a major role. When a society moves toward norms of social responsibility, business is also moving toward the norms, whether consciously or not. The business sector is a part of the social structure where norms influence the behavior of its social actors. When social expectations are heightened, legislation is considered, further intensifying social expectation. The importance of norms and social expectations were well discussed by Himmelstein and Galaskiewicz.

Major reasons against social responsibility are: profit maximization, lack of social skills, costs of social involvement, and a weakened international balance of payment. The idea of profit maximization is the most sound and persuasive argument against social responsibility. It says that a business function is an

economic one. Friedman, the most influential theorist against social responsibility says as follows:

> *In a free enterprise, private property system, a corporate executive is an*
> *employee of the owners of the business. He has direct responsibility to his*
> *employers. That responsibility is to conduct the business in accordance with*
> *their desires, which generally will be to make as much money as possible while*
> *conforming to the basic rules of the society, both those embodied in law and*
> *those embodied in ethical custom. . . . Insofar as his actions in accord with his*
> *social responsibility reduce returns to stockholders, he is spending their money.*
> *Insofar as his actions raise the price to customers, he is spending the customers'*
> *money. Insofar as his actions lower the wages of some employees, he is spending*
> *their money (Friedman, 1971).*

In this argument, when business pursues only profit maximization, it
is making its highest contribution to the society. This argument, however,
gradually lost its persuasiveness as social expectation for corporate social
responsibility intensified in society. Also, many accounts indicate that profit
maximization often leads to corporate behavior that affects society nega-
tively, the cost of which must be borne by everyone.

A lack of social skills is another argument against social responsibility in
business. The focus and training of managers are economic, and as such, they
do not have the necessary skills needed to solve social problems. However,
this argument is also not persuasive anymore because corporations have accumulated the knowledge and skills required to run philanthropic projects.
Alternatively, if they do not have these skills, they can participate in philanthropy through non-profit organizations or hire trained professionals.

Another reason against social responsibility is the costs of social involvement. When companies engage in social obligations, they have to channel
their resources into an area which does not improve economic competitiveness. This might drive out many companies that are marginally surviving.
This argument is still an important consideration for many companies, especially small ones that do not have adequate financial resources. The intangible
nature of the benefits philanthropy may offer makes these companies shy
away from participating in it.

The final argument against social responsibility is a weakened international balance of payments. When U. S. companies have to engage in social
responsibility, it will increase the price of products. If other countries do
not engage in social responsibility, the U. S. companies cannot compete in
the world. Therefore, this argument suggests that social responsibility is
detrimental to the country's economy and consequently to society itself.
As globalization accelerates, multi-national corporations act as if no border

exists. In an age such as this, the argument of an international balance of payments becomes less relevant. Davis' clarification of the debate for and against social responsibility contributed to subsequent studies in the field. Since Davis' time, the social environment on corporate social responsibility has changed drastically. Death and severe illness caused by pollution made judiciary point out the responsibility of the corporations that emitted the harmful materials. More recently, the issue of global warming has pressured many corporations into being more responsible for society and the environment. Generally, the environmental movements since the 1970s have transformed both people's and nation's expectations for corporations to behave in a more socially responsible manner. Thus, ideas against corporate social responsibility are on the wane.

There has always been a struggle to define the concept of social responsibility throughout the history of studying this subject. As the debate between pro corporate social responsibility and anti corporate social responsibility was settled in favor of pro corporate social responsibility, research had shifted to the investigation of "what is corporate social responsibility?"

An influential business scholar in this field is Carroll, who clarified the concept by identifying components of corporate social responsibility. In his discussion, corporate social responsibility and corporate citizenship are almost the same. Carroll (1998) identifies four aspects of corporate social responsibility: economic, legal, ethical and philanthropic. The economic dimension of corporate citizenship is the most basic one for a corporation. Corporations have to be profitable to stay in business: their goal is to maximize sales revenue and minimize costs. Without maintaining this goal, corporations are doomed to fail. The legal dimension of corporate citizenship is also a requirement for corporations, who must obey laws and adhere to regulations such as environmental laws, consumer laws and laws protecting employees. When violated, corporations receive sanctions. The ethical dimension of corporate citizenship comes next. Society expects businesses to fulfill this responsibility, yet it is not a legal requirement of businesses. In this dimension, obeying laws is a minimal behavior, and corporate behavior is expected to exceed this minimal requirement. For example, there are many practices that while not violating laws are ethically questionable, and corporations are expected to avoid these questionable practices. The final dimension of corporate citizenship is philanthropic responsibility. This is the highest level of responsibility that corporations strive for and this is the responsibility that is the focus of corporate citizenship or corporate social responsibility in literature. As the responsibility is desired by society, corporations make monetary contributions to community development, community improvement programs, youth development programs and so forth. They also encourage their workers to

participate in community programs as volunteers. In this case, volunteer time
is paid for by the corporations. The third and fourth dimensions (ethical and
philanthropic) are not forced but are anticipated to meet the expectations. So,
firms' embracement of these dimensions is highly conditional to the social
norms of each society. Carroll's concept of the four dimensions of corporate
citizenship became a benchmark for defining the concept of corporate social
responsibility and generated research to operationalize or empirically measure the concept (Aupperle, 1982 and Pinkston, 1996).

Aupperle (1982) studied corporate social responsibility based on Carroll's
concept of the four dimensions of corporate social responsibility. In clarify-
ing the concept, Aupperle parallels Maslow's hierarchy of needs to Carroll's
four dimensions of corporate social responsibility. Maslow's hierarchy of
needs represents the micro motivations of individuals, categorizing them,
from a low to high level, into five groups of needs: physiological, safety and
security, belongingness, esteem, and self-actualization. The higher needs
are not important until the lower level of needs is fulfilled. The lowest level,
being physiological need, is the most basic requirement for people to live,
and includes food and clothing. If this need is not met, people cannot afford
to seek other needs. However, once this need is fulfilled, the needs move
up a level to that of safety and security, and it is reasonable to assume that
all people like to live in comfortable housing and need a safe environment.
From here, needs move up another level to belongingness. People feel comfortable being with friends and family, and long to be a part of a community.
The fourth level is esteem. People want to be respected by family, friends,
and community, and in contemporary societies in developed nations, people
try to achieve this need. Lastly, the highest level of need, self-actualization,
is reached. In this level, people are satisfied with being themselves, and
so is the highest goal for people and is the level in which people are most
satisfied with their life.

Aupperle sees Carroll's conception of corporate social responsibility as
having a similar hierarchy to organizational responsibility—a macro motivation of society. From lower order to higher order, they are economic, legal,
ethical and discretionary (philanthropic). Again, in this conception, Aupperle
argues that lower order needs have to be fulfilled before higher order needs
are carried out. Therefore, a company has to be profitable before it participates in charity. As a society becomes more advanced, the higher level order
will replace the lower level order in motivating expectations, and therefore,
in a developed society, people expect companies to engage in social matters. In other words, the social expectation of a higher level order permeates
throughout society, and corporations have to respond to the social expectations regardless of their profitability.

Based on Carroll's conception, Aupperle developed his original measurement, which he applied in a study of 818 firms from the 1981 Forbes Annual Directory. A series of factor analyses on the 80 item instrument confirmed Carroll's model of corporate social responsibility. Further, his analyses showed that there is an inverse relationship between the economic and ethical dimensions, indicating that the emphasis on the economic component is at the expense of the ethical component and vice versa.

Pinkston also empirically studied corporate social responsibility adopting Carroll's concept (Pinkston and Carroll, 1994, 1996). Using the instrument developed by Aupperle and Blake, they compared U.S. corporations with companies of six countries-of-origin in America. These countries are England, France, Germany, Japan, Sweden and Switzerland. Because of cultural factors, it was expected that there might be some differences on the perceptions of corporate social responsibility among companies with different countries-of-origin. They looked at four dimensions of corporate citizenship: orientations, organizational stakeholders, issues, and decision-making autonomy. To study the orientations of corporate social responsibility, Carroll's four dimensions of corporate social responsibility were used. For the dimension of organizational stakeholders, owners, consumers, employees, communities, and government are measured. The researchers used 16 items for corporate citizenship issues. They are:

1. Employee health and safety in the workplace
2. Representation/participation of minorities
3. Job security of employees
4. Payment of a fair living wage
5. Protection of personal privacy
6. Environmental protection
7. Contributions to philanthropy
8. Community outreach programming
9. Employees volunteerism
10. Minority development
11. Regulatory compliance
12. Political action contributions
13. Adaptation to local business practices
14. Local government incentives
15. Representation in Washington, D.C.
16. "Grass-roots" lobbying.

For corporate decision-making autonomy, they used a 5-point Likert type scale on which "1" indicates sole subsidiary decision making responsibility and "5" indicates sole headquarter decision making responsibility. The other numbers measure something between these extremes. A sample of 100 firms with foreign headquarters and 191 firms with U.S. headquarters in the U.S. chemical industry from the international directory of corporate affiliations 1990/1991 was used for this research. A survey questionnaire was mailed to these companies with a response rate of 22 percent.

The findings show that the orientations, organizational stakeholders, and issues of corporate social responsibility are not significantly different among corporations of different countries-of-origin. The only significant difference was found in the decision-making autonomy of corporate social responsibility. The U.S. companies have the least decision-making autonomy. That is, the headquarters of U.S. companies have more power than their subsidiaries in deciding the course of business actions compared to companies from England, France, Germany, Japan, Sweden and Switzerland. In contrast, Swedish companies have the most decision-making autonomy among companies from the other countries-of-origin. In the case of Japan and the U.S. comparison, this result can be interpreted by the lack of philanthropic experiences of Japanese corporations in the United States. Since they do not have such experiences, the headquarters in Japan have to rely on local subsidiaries which employ Americans who are more familiar with philanthropy.

Carroll's four dimensions of corporate social responsibility lists all responsibilities that a company has to take in society. Therefore, it is more encompassing than the common notion of corporate citizenship, in which only philanthropy or charity are mentioned. Pinkston's concept of corporate social responsibility is much wider than Carroll's. For example, the dimension of organizational stakeholders in corporate social responsibility includes all actors—owners, employees and governments are included. This is more than the common notion of stakeholders in corporate citizenship as only the community. Studies summarized here indicate business and organizational scholars' tendency to focus on corporate social responsibility in relation to profit making, the core business function of enterprises. This is in contrast to the sociological approaches of corporate social responsibility which look at the social origin of corporate social responsibility and its wider relations with other aspects of society.

COMPARATIVE APPROACHES TO CORPORATE SOCIAL RESPONSIBILITY

Although Pinkston and Carroll saw the importance of cultural factors that affect the performance of corporate social responsibility, their study did not show a detailed description of the difference. This is partly due to their choice of quantitative methods, which tend to lose contextual information. In this sense, research by Bob and his associates (1990) allows us to understand the differences between the U.S. and Japanese corporations on corporate citizenship. Their study shows how Japanese corporations view and engage in corporate philanthropy. Japanese firms see corporate citizenship as deeply rooted in American society, going back to the era of American frontier. During the frontier expansion, local and national governments barely functioned, leading to the formation of communities by and for the citizens. The importance of community resided in the creation of civic associations within communities, which served a variety of needs. The idea of community has become so important in the American tradition that it has affected the subsequent development of corporations and the governments. In the contemporary idea of corporate citizenship, enlightened self-interest became the backbone of the concept. This means that individuals and corporations do not engage in charities and other philanthropic tasks solely for altruistic reasons. Instead, their engagement involves the pursuit of eventual returns. For example, a donation to a local school will improve the quality of the local labor force. The generation of this concept presented more opportunities for corporations to participate in philanthropy because they were able to explain it is an investment. To spend money on philanthropy, corporate managers needed to have accountability.

Based on the experiences of American companies, Bob and his associates developed a model of corporate citizenship that is centered on the relationship between corporation and community. In this model, corporate citizens have five resources to improve five areas of community life. The first resource corporations can use is philanthropy, through which they can donate money to community events, projects and programs, and this is the most common resource companies usually use. The second resource is in-kind donations, which is often used by corporations that do not have money to spend. In-kind donations include donating employees' time, company products, corporate expertise (e.g., financial analysis) or corporate services (e.g., printing service). The third resource is corporate leadership and prestige, which can bring more support and money from outside the community. For example, when a prestigious company in a community supports a cause to improve the community, other community groups are more likely to support it. The fourth resource is human resources, especially human resource decisions and policies. For example, companies can hire women and minorities or, their day care services can be used by the community residents. The fifth resource is the company's external business relationships. This means that companies can use their external operating decisions for the benefit of the community. A

company may bring their parts company to the community, bringing with it
more jobs. Likewise, they can invest in local companies which are strength
ening their capital.

These resources of corporate citizens are targeted to five areas of community life. If they can improve these five areas, the quality of life in a
community will also improve. The first area is arts and culture. Corporations
can support arts and culture in a community such as museums or public
radio. In Japan, support for arts and culture is a dominant form of corporate
philanthropy. In the United States, many national and local corporations donate money to National Public Radio and it is a way to spread corporations'
names. The second area is education and training, such as supporting local
schools or creating scholarships. Creating a scholarship that was named after
a company or the founder of the company is a well-known practice. The third
area is health and human services, where firms can support community health
care or child care, or help homeless people. The fourth area is community development. Examples are improving public facilities, parks, and housing, etc.
Community development can be divided into two areas: capacity building of
people and the building of infrastructure. The first area focuses on processes,
and is difficult to assess the results. Therefore, corporate participation in
community development tends to be the latter one. The final area is economic development. This may include downtown development or improving
technological capacity in local firms. As for-profit organizations, firms have
excelled in this last area of community life, and this is where they can expect
to receive tangible benefits. Corporate citizens can improve these five areas
of community life using companies' five resources.

Bob and his associates argue that Japanese corporations define corporate
citizenship differently from the American model. Japanese views of corporate
citizenship are far narrower than American views. For Japanese, corporate
citizenship means providing stable jobs and paying taxes. From the perspective of Japanese firms, the five areas of community life just mentioned are
usually taken care of by the government and/or families, that is, these areas
are in the realm of government and families, not corporations. However,
in Japan and overseas, Japanese companies have gradually redefined their
concept of corporate citizenship. As many developed nations, including the
United States, expect the fulfillment of corporate citizenship roles, this redefi-
nition is necessary for Japanese corporations to be successful in the global
business climate. The rapid development of information technology spreads
companies' reputation for either good or bad around the world instantly. So,
if a society in which Japanese corporations have directly invested has social
expectations of active corporate philanthropy, they have to adopt that culture
for success.

A survey by Bob and his associates shows the necessity of Japanese companies engaging in community activities. Eighty-nine percent of Americans in the study think that Japanese companies in the United States should be involved in local communities at least equal to the level of American companies. Japanese companies are very sensitive about what Americans' think about them. When Japan has had a trade surplus and Japanese companies bought real estate in America, Americans worried about the economic power of Japan. There were rallies and buyers' strikes. The U.S. government also pressured Japan for more balanced bilateral trade. The Japanese government and companies tried to reduce the friction between the countries, and corporate citizenship has been one strategy for reducing this friction, at least at the local community level.

As Ostrander and Schervish have identified, philanthropy is mainly based on morals and norms. Therefore, it is important to touch upon business ethics in Japan. Taka's article (1997) is a good overview of the Japanese business ethic. He defines business ethics as a discipline which studies the relationships between economic activities and the realization of fairness in societies and economic practices, as well as activities that contribute to the realization of fairness in societies. He shows five stages of business ethics development in Japan. The first stage is the period before the mid-1960s. In December 27, 1960, Prime Minister, Hayato Ikeda's cabinet decided on an economic policy that would double GNP in 10 years, from 13 trillion yen to 26 trillion yen. Thus, the priority of the Japanese government and business was economic growth. Japan showed phenomenal economic growth, and within 7 years their goal was achieved. During this period, there was no room for corporations to deal with social and environmental issues, and the government was reluctant to deal with it.

The second stage is a period between the mid-1960s and mid-70s. This is when the negative aspects of the rapid economic growth began to emerge, and in this stage, social issues became an important factor for business. For example, environmental cases such as Minamata disease[1] ended in favor of the plaintiffs, who sued the companies for compensation. Together with Minamata disease, other environmental problems such as Niigata Minamata disease in Niigata prefecture in 1965 (mercury poisoning caused by Showa Electrical Works) and Yokkaichi Asthma caused by air pollution in Yokkaichi city, Mie prefecture, in 1961 frightened Japanese people. Many anti-pollution movements took place to help the victims and accuse companies and the government. These environmental problems and the resulting anti-pollution movements made it clear that corporations are responsible for the consequences of their production processes, and a government that did not regulate corporate activities is also accountable for the problem. Therefore, in this stage, the government as well as businesses learned that they had to take social issues seriously. In 1970, the winter Diet session, the so called "Pollution Diet session," passed 14 anti-pollution laws and made a significant amendment to the Basic Law for Environmental Pollution Control, which was originally enacted in 1967. The amendment solely emphasized the maintenance of the environment in which people live, as well as economic development, which was emphasized in the original law. In 1971, the Environmental Agency, a sub-cabinet level governmental agency, was established to solve the environmental problems.

The third stage occurred in the second half of the 1970s. Due to the oil crisis, many corporations were restructuring and abandoning their role in social responsibility. For them, simple survival was of primary importance, and many did not have enough financial strength to consider the secondary business function of corporate social responsibility. They had to focus on their primary business function of profit making. The government also became reluctant to enhance stricter environmental regulations.

The fourth stage took place in the 1980s, the time of the bubble economy. Stock and land prices continued to increase, and people spent money for luxurious items generously. Japanese business leaders thought their management style was superior—more efficient and therefore more ethical, but this did not necessarily lead to a return to a social responsibility role. Corporations spent money for speculation in stocks and land in addition to capital investment for expansion.

The fifth stage occurred in the 1990s. In this stage, two trends can be detected, both negative and positive. On the positive side, major business associations took a leading role in philanthropic activities (e.g., Keidanren's Committee on Corporate Philanthropy and Doyukai's Corporate Citizenship Committee). These associations guided major corporations' course of action. On the negative side, the Japanese business community cannot clear up illicit political donations and *dango* (bid-rigging) practices completely. It is hard to get rid of them because they are rooted in the Japanese way of business. The alliance of bureaucracy, business and the ruling Liberal Democratic Party has been a mechanism in which Japan's direction was planned and implemented. Illicit political donations and *dango* practices were parts of this mechanism. Taka's five stages of business ethic development shows economic and social events have influenced the characteristics of the development of corporate social responsibility.

The literature reviewed here suggests that corporate social responsibility is an integral part of the American way of doing business. It is an idea developed by the unique history of America, where independence from the government has a strong appeal. Although corporate social responsibility has had important roles in Japanese society, it is not as widely recognized or embraced by businesses as in the United States. Socio-cultural influences are the key factors to understand the difference in corporate social responsibility. When Japanese corporations move to the United States for operations, however, they have to deal with this issue. Companies that adopted corporate citizenship roles during the bubble economy in Japan might be more active in the United States. Also, firm characteristics, such as company philosophy and identity, may interact to affect patterns of Japanese companies' performance on corporate social responsibility. In a sense, this study tries to understand how Japanese companies have dealt with the American way of corporate social responsibility.

INSTITUTIONAL THEORY IN ORGANIZATIONS LITERATURE

Institutional theory has gained popularity in organizational literature in recent years as one of the prospective paradigms to understand the relationships between organizations and the environment. As such, organizations are viewed as open systems: Organizations are properly understood by studying their wider social and cultural contexts. In a sense, institutional theory looks at the wider contexts and their influences on organizations.

Scott (1995) reviewed a considerable number of studies on institutions and institutional theories, and subsequently identifies three analytically distinct structures within institutions: regulative, normative, and cognitive. These structures constrain or support individual organizations, and as such, institutions are very important for each organization's maintenance and growth. According to Scott, institutions are defined as "consisting of cognitive, normative, and regulative structures and activities that provide stability and meaning to social behavior. Institutions are transported by various carriers— cultures, structures, and routines—and they operate at multiple levels of jurisdiction (1995:33)." The three structures of institutions are useful for categorizing the variety of studies related to them.

The regulative structure of an institution gives attention to explicit regulative processes of rule-setting, monitoring, and sanctioning activities. The regulative processes can be conducted formally through law enforcement or informally through people shaming or shunning. In the regulative structure, coercion is the main control mechanism. Therefore, the actors (individual organizations) follow the rules or regulations whether they agree or not. If they do not follow the rules, they face sanctions. Violating rules often costs the organizations more than obeying the rules. Many studies from this perspective look at the state as a key actor and see the relationship between the state and organizations. Because corporate social responsibility is not required by laws, formal negative sanctions on corporations for their behavior do not exist. Therefore, corporations can do business without any involvement in corporate social responsibility. Many corporations in the United States engage in philanthropy proactively in order to avoid government creating laws pertaining to corporate social responsibility, which would bind corporate action. Formal positive sanctions to corporations are observed when we look at the tax exemption on corporate giving. This encourages corporations to participate in corporate social responsibility, such as donating to charity and reducing activities which emit carbon dioxide. At times, the government may change its formal positive sanctions to negative positive sanctions as social expectation changes. For example, as the international community asks the state for more efforts to reduce carbon dioxide emissions, the government may change its policy from tax incentives to mandatory measures.

Looking at institutions from the normative perspective is an old and basic approach in sociology. For example, Durkheim, Parsons and Selznick conceived the institutions as normative. Values and norms are the basic components of institutions: values are people's conception of what is beneficial and important, while norms are patterns of behavior relating to how things should be done. Therefore, normative structure defines the goals or purposes of organizations and individuals in addition to how their goals are achieved. Those values and norms are represented by roles; which specify the appropriate and expected behaviors for individuals or organizations. As with the regulative structure, the normative structure constrains actor's behavior. An actor's behaviors are narrowed down to certain acceptable behaviors by society. However, the normative structure has the internalized element for each individual and organization, and as such, has an enabling aspect in the actor's behavior. While the regulative structure imposes its directives on individuals and organizations and they grudgingly follow the orders, the normative structure allows them to behave more actively. When the idea is internalized, actions will be voluntary, rather than forced. From the perspective of the normative structure, we can analyze corporations' philanthropic behaviors by paying attention to what kinds of social norms encourage corporations to participate in the activities, and by comparing a corporation with other companies and the community. An example of the latter is an investigation of active participation in corporate giving by the neighboring companies, which may influence a company's corporate decision on how much to give.

The emphasis on the cognitive structure of institutions is the most recent approach, and has been developed partly as the discerning characteristic of the new institutionalism, or neo-institutional theory, within sociology. In this theoretical tradition, symbols and cultures that motivate actions are treated as objective and external to social actors. So, the cognitive structure of institutions has a close affinity to the social constructionist approach, which strengthened the symbolic interactionism, emphasizing the subjective and internal meanings of social actions. Thus, the idea of cognitive structure on institutions has a close relationship with social theorists such as Blumer, Goffman and Berger, who lean to agency in understanding society. Therefore, while the normative aspect emphasizes the structural side of institutions, the cognitive aspect focuses more on the agency side of institutions. The cognitive aspect allows us to see "mediating between the external world of stimuli and the response of the individual organism is a collection of internalized symbolic representation of the world (Scott, 1995: 40)." The objective world can be understood as taken for granted because it is so fundamental to actors' daily life, yet it is a social construction of reality through ongoing interaction. In this structure, corporate social responsibility can be seen as necessary for business operation. That reality is formed by interacting with non-profit organizations, business partners and local people. Once corporate social responsibility is recognized as a business strategy, it can be used to build a good corporate image and public relationship.

Neo-institutional theory grants actors more of an agency role compared with regulative and normative structures. In regulative structures, individuals and organizations are passive in their behavior, forced to obey the rules. They may act in accordance with the regulations regardless of their preferences. On the other hand, in the normative structures, actors internalize their roles in a socialization process. They can act with their own will. However, the choice of action has been circumscribed by the norms of society. In contrast, in cognitive structures, the choice itself can be constructed by actors. Therefore, cognitive structures grant the most positive role to actors, and regulative structures give the most passive role to actors.

In the cognitive perspective, the idea of social identity is an important concept to understand the actions of individuals and organizations. Whereas social roles are the guiding principle of actions in the normative perspective, social identity is the guiding principle of actions in the cognitive perspective. Social identity is "our conceptions of who we are and what ways of action make sense for us in a given situation (Scott, 1995:44)." By identifying ourselves as who we are, we will take actions that are appropriate and satisfactory to that identification. When the individuals and organizations face uncertainty, they try to imitate others with whom they share similar social identity, and who have superior or successful performance. In other words, in times of uncertainty, they mimic the actions of better individuals and organizations so that they can hope to reduce that uncertainty. The mimetic processes of organizations and individuals are survival strategies for them. The cognitive perspective sees them as important components of institutionalization.

The institutional theory provides many insights about the philanthropic activities of Japanese firms. As Carroll's conception of corporate social responsibility indicates, philanthropy is separate from the legal aspect of the corporate social responsibility. Therefore, the analytical category of the regulative structure of institutions may not be so helpful to understand philanthropy. The normative and cognitive structures of institutions will be the main theoretical orientation for this study. It is assumed that Japanese firms try to create an identity for themselves when they come to the United States. That is, they may want to become an American company with American management and operation styles, or they may want to remain as a Japanese company. Their identification will be consciously shaped by pursuing the best corporate practice that increases the chance for survival in a foreign land. It will guide the course of action in corporate social responsibility accordingly. Also, they learn what is expected of them in order to be successful in American society. In this study of corporate citizenship, the normative and cognitive aspects may not be clearly distinguished, as Scott (1995) describes. His categorization of institutions having three structures is an analytical tool. However, in empirical research, the interdependence, complementariness and ambiguity of the distinctions of the regulative, normative and cognitive structures of institutions cannot be overlooked (Dacin, 1997:822).

NOTE

1. Minamata disease was discovered in Minamata city, Kumamoto Prefecture, Japan, in 1956, and later in Niigata city, Niigata Prefecture, Japan, in 1965. Methyl mercury from factories had accumulated in fish and shellfish. Residents who ate those fish and shellfish were subsequently poisoned with it. There are 3,000 officially recognized Minamata disease patients and 12,000 more people are suspected of Minamata disease. The symptoms of Minamata disease are sensory disturbance, constriction of the visual field, coordination disturbance, dysarthria, hearing disturbance, tremor and walking disturbance (Harada, 1999)

Chapter Three

Research Method

CASE STUDY

The nature of the research questions determines what kind of a research method we will use. In other words, what we want to know guides us to what kind of research method best answers the questions. In this study, the author is mainly interested in the level and nature of the corporate social responsibility of Japanese manufacturing companies in Kentucky in comparison to those in the United States. After reviewing the literature on Japanese corporate social responsibility outside Japan, it is clear that there are not many studies or discussions about this issue. At present, and to the best of the author's knowledge, there is no study that investigates Japanese corporate philanthropy that is contextualized within an American community in a comparative perspective. Hence, it is difficult to have a formal hypothesis or *modus operandi* that is typically used in quantitative research, such as surveys. This study is exploratory in nature, therefore, a case study was chosen as the best method for this research.

The purpose of this study is to explore the social phenomenon of the corporate social responsibility of Japanese firms in America. As a research area, it is important to understand the phenomenon comprehensively, for this can help future research on this topic. It clarifies what are the issues in the topic. Here, the clarification of issues means that it identifies problems that are pertinent to sociological theories and concepts. That is, the phenomenon under investigation can help to refine our understanding of sociological theories and concepts. For example, the phenomenon regarding the corporate philanthropy of Japanese manufacturing companies in the United States can support or help to understand the adaptation theory or/and institutional theory. Alternatively, this phenomenon may indicate the limitation of these theories.

Also, the clarification of issues is important in applied sociology, which is a
discipline that uses sociological knowledge for the betterment of society and
the community. In this case, by understanding the nature of Japanese corporate philanthropy better, community leaders and non-profit organizations can
solicit more support from Japanese corporations. They need to understand the
cultural background of the Japanese people and their firms to effectively request donations. Also, Japanese corporations can better understand the nature
of American philanthropy and how to get involved in the activity. This will
be a critical factor for them in order to reduce conflict with the community in
which they establish facilities.

Case studies of multiple data sources allow us to understand the phenomenon with depth and comprehensiveness. Importantly, the research also
raises the question of how Japanese firms may alter their processes in order
to adapt to the American norms of corporate social responsibility. When
studying a process, a case study method has some advantages over survey
methods. For example, in a cross sectional survey, data is gathered at one
point in time. Therefore, it cannot capture the process, but rather, represents
a frozen moment of the phenomenon. Also, in a time series survey, data is
gathered at two or more points in time, so it can show the changes over
time. However, it cannot capture the process. It remains as snapshots of
the phenomenon at two or more points in time. In other words, it does not
tell us what is going on between the two points. Another reason to choose
a case study method is that this process of adaptation of corporate social
responsibility norms is not well known, and therefore, to construct a survey
questionnaire is difficult. Survey questions need a clear definition and operationalization of concepts.

The case study approach is a widely used method in social sciences. Yin
(1989) defines a case study as "an empirical inquiry that: investigates a contemporary phenomenon within its real-life context; when the boundaries between phenomenon and context are not clearly evident; and multiple sources
of evidence are used (p.23)." It is often categorized as qualitative research
(Leedy, 1997; Stake, 1998), however, it can be both qualitative and quantitative (Yin, 1989; Hartley, 1994). For example, several case studies (Pressman
& Wildavsky, 1973; Pelz, 1981; both cited by Yin, 1989) coded data into
numerical form for analyses.

A case study can be used for three research purposes, namely, exploration,
description and explanation (Yin, 1989). In an exploratory study, it investigates phenomena that have not been studied or are not well known. When
the phenomenon is not well known, it is difficult to separate the phenomenon
from the context. In this circumstance, a survey or experiment is not suitable.
A case study is a better choice in this regard. It is also a better option for a

descriptive study. For its purpose, a study must delineate many aspects of the phenomenon comprehensively. A case study using multiple data gathering procedures can assure the collection of comprehensive data. The method is also used for explanatory purposes. When properly analyzed, data from case studies can establish causal relationships. Pattern-matching is a dominant mode of analytic strategy (Yin, 1989). It compares an empirically based pattern with a predicted one, and thus, when the patterns match each other, can confirm the causal relationship.

In a case study, there are mainly six strategies of data collection (Yin, 1989). They are: documentation, archival records, interviews, direct observations, participant-observation, and physical artifacts. Examples of documentation are to utilize personal letters, minutes of meetings, newspapers, etc. Data from documents is used to corroborate the argument pursued or to refute the counter arguments. Archival records include maps and charts, organizational records, service records, etc. The relevance of the archival records varies depending on the subject of study. The interview is the most important source of data as it captures the thought processes and experiences of informants. Usually, interviews are conducted with key informants, and two types of questions, open-ended and structured questions, are possible. Direct observation supports the argument developed by other data. For example, an observation of a run-down neighborhood can bolster the concept of lower class status, which is indicated by interviews. Participant-observation is an instance in which a researcher is a part of the phenomenon under investigation. This strategy is also a major mode of data collection. Physical artifacts such as tools and furniture can be a data source. However, these data are not as relevant as the data from other sources, such as interviews and participant observations. In a case study, a combination of these data collection strategies is used to understand/explain a social phenomenon.

A major strength of a case study method is the richness of the data collected and analyzed compared to quantitative methods, such as a survey. Multiple data sources allow us to describe phenomena deeply. In addition, a case study can capture the processes underlying the phenomenon. Suppose one wants to study the increase of a company's giving. If one uses a survey method, one could send a questionnaire to the company executives asking why they increased the amount of the giving. Hence, one could understand the reasons for giving, but may have difficulty in knowing how they arrived at the decision. However, in a case study method, it is possible to learn the process of decision-making (e.g., negotiations among executives and influences from non-profit organizations in the community). A case study is good for issues where phenomena and the context cannot be separated easily. Therefore, it is often used for theory-generating research.

A limitation of this method is its weak generalizability. This is a critique from researchers of quantitative methods. They claim that since it is based on a case, or several cases, it cannot be generalized. In response to this critique, researchers who use case studies argue that a case study is generalizable to the propositions, and that they are not generalizing to the population (Yin, 1989). Also, Stake (1998) argues that a case study can help to establish the limits of generalizability (p. 104). So, it is understood that a case study is not suitable for research that needs to generalize to the population. The important point is to know what the purpose of study is first. Then, we will choose a method or methods that are appropriate for the purpose.

The lengthy discussion on the case study approach above is intended to persuade the reader that the approach chosen for this research is the most suitable. In general, this study is exploratory in nature. Because of insufficient studies conducted on the topic, the purpose of the study will be to understand the phenomenon. Company philosophy and its influence on the nature and level of corporate philanthropy will be explored. Also, how Japanese companies learn about corporate giving, which is a foreign concept for many Japanese, will be investigated. One of interesting topics in this study is the possible relationship between firm size and corporate philanthropy. Except for a few studies, not much research has been conducted on this topic in the case of Japanese corporations. However, more research has been conducted in the case of American corporations. Using existing findings and arguments, whether a relationship exists between firm size and the level of corporate giving will be explored. This part of the research can be considered as explanatory research. Although it is not as rigorous as survey or experimental types of research methods, case studies can also be used for explanatory studies (Yin, 1989). Causal relationships can be demonstrated using pattern-matching, and this can be useful in comparing an empirically based pattern with a predicted one. In this case, data from interviews and organizational records is compared with the findings and arguments of former research. This will allow us to assess the existence/non-existence of the relationship.

SELECTION OF A COMMUNITY

A list of Japanese companies by community was used to select a community to be studied. The list was compiled using data from the Kentucky Cabinet for Economic Development (1999). As of 1999, there were 109 Japanese corporations located in 39 communities in the Commonwealth of Kentucky (see Appendix. A). These 39 communities became candidates for the final research community, the selection of which was a process of elimination. Large communities were the first to be eliminated from consideration, due to the fact that the populations of communities such as Louisville and Lexington, which have population of around 250,000, are too large to capture the inter-action between community and corporation. Also, communities with minor numbers of local employees within Japanese companies were eliminated, because this small number makes it difficult to ascertain what, if any, impact the Japanese companies have on the community. A variation in number of employees is another consideration. In some communities, there are 3 or 4 Japanese companies. However, their numbers of employees are at the same level. These communities are deleted from the deliberation. When these fac-tors are taken into consideration, only a few communities are left. Then, the existence of comparable American corporations in terms of size and type of industry was considered. In this process of elimination, Heartland[1] was found to have comparable size and type of American industries and therefore it was selected for the research site.

Heartland has three Japanese companies with employment of 50, 674 and 1,700. One of the companies, Kagoshima, is a flagship of the Japanese economy, and well-known for its corporate citizenship role in Japan and over-seas. The other two companies are not so well-known. Heartland has many American firms with comparable number of employees, and therefore, there appears little issue with comparing Japanese and American firms on corporate citizenship in this community.

Although it was initially not a consideration, it was later discovered that Heartland is a very active community in philanthropy. This was an important factor for this research. If a community was chosen that had a relatively inactive role in philanthropy, it would be impossible to observe any kind of philanthropic activities by Japanese corporations. The literature review from Himmelstein (1996) and Bob et al (1990) as reviewed in the previous chapter showed that corporate philanthropy is a foreign concept for Japanese. This suggests that when a community does not have an active role in philanthropy, Japanese companies in the community may also be less likely to be philan-thropically active. Fortunately, this was not the case in Heartland.

For the purposes of this exploratory study, it was sufficient to research only a single community, because the unit of analysis is organization, as opposed to community or the individuals in a company. What needed to be investi-gated in this study is the behavior of Japanese corporations in philanthropic activities in Kentucky. In other words, this study seeks to explore firm spe-cific corporate philanthropy. There was a concern that the interaction between a community and corporations may differ by community context. In the early years of Japanese direct investment to the Commonwealth of Kentucky, there were some resentment, due to the possible environmental pollution and the

legality of incentive packages connected to the investments (Yanarella and
Reid, 1990). If they still exist in communities, the interaction with Japanese
companies is different from the communities where they welcome Japanese
direct investment. Therefore, the community context before selecting the
community was reviewed. For the purpose of this research, community
context is defined as the degree of the community's acceptance of Japanese investment. In other words, the community may welcome Japanese
factories and Japanese expatriates into the community, or the community
may be resentful of accepting Japanese factories and people. In order to see
how Kentucky communities see Japanese direct investment, the Lexington
Herald Leader and the Kentucky Post were surveyed between October 1995
and April 1999. It was found that 31 articles were related to Japanese direct
investment, and among those, 26 articles reflected the positive aspects of
Japanese investments. Two headlines read: "Toyota's Corporate Citizenship
Good for Business" (Kentucky Post, December 5, 1995), and "85 Wheel
Deal Drove Decade of Big Changes: Chain of Positive Effects in Bluegrass
Muted Debate Over Toyota Incentives" (Lexington Herald Reader, December 10, 1995). On the other hand, only three articles were negative. Two of
them dealt with a Japanese company (Far East Tools Engineering Inc.) were
allegedly polluting Owenton (Kentucky Post, March 14, 1996; Lexington
Herald Reader, March 7, 1996). Another negative article was an analysis
of the social impact of a growing Japanese population. The Kentucky Post
read: "Influx of Japanese Forces Schools to Adapt (Erlanger)" (Kentucky
Post, November 12, 1996). Two other articles were neutral about Japanese
investment. Looking at these results, it is felt that almost all Kentucky
communities welcome Japanese firms. In order to support this impression,
four professors were consulted. Being long-term Kentucky residents, they
had a wealth of knowledge on Kentucky communities, and whether or not
there was hostility towards Japanese investments within them. All of them
said that they did not know of any Kentucky communities hostile to the
Japanese investment. These four experts[2] on Kentucky communities support
the impression.

Also, Hougland's analysis (2001) on the public perception of Toyota in
Kentucky, for which he used data from the Survey Research Center of the
University of Kentucky, supports this expression. The surveys were conducted
with the residents of Scott County, where Toyota is located, and the residents
of eight other adjacent counties in 1986, 1987, 1988, 1989, 1990, 1991, 1993
and 1995. According to the 1995 data, 90.1 percent of Scott County residents
said "the Toyota plant is benefiting the community and its residents." Since
the survey's first year, the percentages have steadily increased. For the resi-

dents of eight other adjacent counties, the percentages were in the range of 70 to 80 between 1986 and 1990. However, for 1993, the most recent year in which data is available, the percentage was 88.4 percent. Based on the data, he concluded that "for the most part, however, central Kentucky's residents appear to be maintaining a favorable image of their communities and developing a favorable image of Toyota and its management (p. 297)."

It is possible that some World War II veterans or others are hostile to the Japanese presence in their communities. Some anecdotal evidence from the city of Middletown, Heartland's adjacent city, suggests that such antagonism is not likely. A World War II army tank sits on a hill nearby a Japanese factory as Bataan War Memorial. It is a memorial for 66 local soldiers who were killed or captured by the Japanese army during the Bataan March in the Philippines during World War II. Despite this unfortunate history, there does not appear to be any resentment toward Japan in the town (Yotsumoto, 2001).

For these reasons, it was decided upon to focus on a single community, considering the community context as it relates to the general acceptance of Japanese investment as a constant. Although the intensive field study focused on a single community, data from field studies in other communities, as well as data from existing research, were utilized for analyzing the social phenomena.

DEFINITIONS OF THE CONCEPTS

Based on the literature reviewed, the definitions below are used for operationalization.

(A). Corporate social responsibility

Refers to explicit actions of a corporation to improve a community. The actions may include direct donations of money, in-kind donations and employees' volunteer work paid for by firms. The actions are targeted to five areas of community life: (1) arts and culture, (2) education and training, (3) health and human services, (4) public facility improvement, and (5) job creation. In this study, corporate social responsibility is the same as corporate citizenship. Amount of money, in-kind donations, and volunteering time spent by a corporation in these five areas of community life can indicate the magnitude of the corporate social responsibility and general level of involvement as a corporate citizen of the community. [This definition is based on Bob and his associates (1990).]

(B). Corporate Giving

This is an element of corporate social responsibility. It is equal to corporation's monetary donation to charity.

(C). A Japanese company

A corporation with ownership of more than 51 percent of shares by Japanese and its headquarters is located in Japan.

(D). An American company

A corporation with ownership of more than 51 percent of shares by Americans and its headquarters is located in the United States.

(E). A British company

A corporation with ownership of more than 51 percent of shares by the British and its headquarters is located in the United Kingdom.

(F). Community

A locality in which people live and interact with each other. For this study, incorporated urban places are used as an operationalization of community.

(G). Corporate Identity

Refers to the intrinsic, self-organizing qualities that constitute actor individuality (Wendt, 1994). In this study, the concept is used in relation to the views on philanthropy.

(H). Corporate Philosophy

This is an element of corporate identity. It is a corporation's collective idea of how to do business.

(I). Firm size

In this study, it is operationalized as a number of employees in a company.

DATA COLLECTION

This study is a result of fieldwork and archival data collection that were conducted between 1999 and 2004. The initial fieldwork was conducted in the fall of 1999, after which the major fieldwork was conducted in the summer of 2000. Some follow-up interviews were then carried out intermittently until early 2004. In addition, archival data collection was carried out throughout the period.

As in case studies, multiple data collection techniques were used. The most important source of data is from interviews: three Japanese firms, two American firms and one British firm in Heartland were selected for this purpose. The three Japanese firms represent all the Japanese firms in Heartland, being large, medium and small in terms of employee numbers. It is important to note that firm size is relative to the size of the community. Large cities, such as Detroit, can have corporate facilities that employ over 10,000 people. However, Heartland's community has a population of only 15,263, and as such, a large size means 1,000–2,000 employees, a medium size equates to a couple of hundreds employees, and a small size means less than 100 employees. The three Japanese firms are Kagoshima, GTS Wire & Cable, and Dainichi, being large, medium, and small respectively. The two American firms represented in the study are B. B. Fishwater and Goodman Incorporated. B. B. Fishwater employs 1,100 people, and is the second largest employer after Kagoshima in the community. Goodman Incorporated employs approximately 100 people. By looking at a list of manufacturing firms in Heartland, there were no American firms comparable to Dainichi, which has approximately 50 employees. Therefore, Goodman Incorporated was chosen as a representative of a small sized American firm. Initially, Fortson Conveyer, which employs about 300 people, was selected as a representative of a medium sized American firm. However, during an interview, it was found that Fortson Conveyer was purchased by a British company, and is therefore considered as a British company located in Heartland.

A letter was sent to these corporations asking for an interview. Due to previous contact with both Kagoshima and Dainichi, they responded to the request immediately, as did Goodman Incorporated and Fortson Conveyers. Due to an error in the initial mail out, in which the previous plant manger's name was attached, B. B. Fishwater responded positively after a second letter was sent with the name of the new plant manager attached. GTS Wire & Cable was difficult to contact, and no response was received from the initial request. However, a second attempt was more successful, and they later agreed to an interview. Interestingly, at that time, all members of Japanese management team had been sent back to Japan, and a new management team had only just arrived. Therefore, they neither had the time to be interviewed, nor the knowledge necessary on the company's philanthropic matters, because they had not yet gone through a full handover from the previous management team.

In addition, the General County Industrial Foundation, General County Community Development Council and Kentucky Bluegrass United Way were contacted for data collection. Data from the General County Industrial Foundation and the General County Community Development Council was obtained to see what kind of views the community leaders have on philanthropy in general, and the contribution of Japanese firms to the community specifically. They were willing to help by responding to requests immediately.

The decision to contact Kentucky Bluegrass United Way was to obtain data so as to assess the views of a recipient of philanthropy, and to corroborate claims made by the companies. This did not work well. A letter to the director of Kentucky Bluegrass United Way requesting an interview was sent, however, the request for an interview was refused by the director because she was in the middle of a fund-raising campaign. As an alternative, a short questionnaire was sent to her, which she provided answers to, as well as some data on corporate giving.

Interviews were conducted with the companies and two agencies mentioned above. They were administered in their offices. The interviewees in the companies are designated representatives, such as presidents, plant managers and human resources managers. The interviewees in each agency were directors. In total, nine in-depth interview sessions were conducted and a total of eleven designated representatives were interviewed. Each interview took from one to one and a half hours. The interview was an open-ended and semi-structured format. Notes were taken during the interviews and they were recorded. In addition, informal conversations with employees in Japanese corporations also proved to be a valuable data source.

Direct observations from visiting a research site provided another data source. For example, at the factories, it was possible to view production processes, which provided a deeper understanding of what they do. It was also possible to note signs that represent corporate citizenship. For example, a plaque from the United Way on the wall shows a willingness to be involved in philanthropy. Archival records from the firms also became a data source, and company brochures and other information were requested. In addition, local history books and websites on the Internet became a valuable data source.

DATA ANALYSIS

Data analysis in qualitative research is sometimes called a creative act (Lofland & Lofland, 1995:181). Many qualitative researchers think that the analysis is an end product of intuition and an emergent process, and because it depends on these, there is no step by step approach for the analysis itself. However, there are several pre-analysis procedures that can help to facilitate the analysis. In this research, the first step was to transcribe the recordings of the interviews. Just listening to interviews may lead one to miss important topics or sentences. Transcripts can allow us to immerse ourselves into the data. Also, this is a prerequisite for the next step. The second step is coding. It is a way of categorizing and sorting data. Lofland and Lofland offer several questions that can help to sort data (1995, 186). These are:

- Of what topic, unit, or aspect is this an instance?
- What question about a topic does this item of data suggest?
- What sort of an answer to a question about a topic does this item of data suggest?
- What does it represent?
- What is this an example of?
- What do I see going on here?

Data is categorized using these questions. Charmaz (1983, 111) mentions two functions of coding in the analysis. First, it serves as shorthand devices to label, separate, compile, and organize data. Second, it serves to summarize, synthesize, and sort many observations made of the data.

For this study, 3 × 5 cards were used, and these were coded by topics, such as firm size. Cards include not only quotations from interviews, but also quotations from existing literature and the author's ideas on the topics. These cards became the basic building blocks for the analysis, along with a strategy called 'concept charting', which includes arranging working elements on a single sheet of paper (Lofland, 1995:198). This strategy helps to clarify what the relationships are among the coded data. Charts and comments were then drawn up in a large sketch pad (18 × 12 inches).

LIMITATIONS OF THIS STUDY

There are three concerns relating to the quality of this study. First is the unit of analysis, which is the corporate organization, in which some attempt is made to understand how corporations behave in philanthropy. However, as data was mainly collected from individuals who are designated representatives, it was difficult to ascertain whether or not the opinion was a collective company one, or that of the individual, leading to a potential pitfall in the analysis. Two things can be said here that help to reduce this concern. First, clarification on the source of the opinion can be sought during the interviews. Second, because they are designated representatives of each company, their opinions shape the course of the company. Although attention was paid to this issue during data collection, care must be taken when later analyzing the interview data.

The second concern is a revelation that one of the selected firms had been acquired by a British company. Initially, the research was designed to include three American companies with small, medium and large sizes, so that it can be compared to Japanese firms of similar size. However, due to the British takeover of Fortson Conveyers, there was no longer a medium sized American firm represented. This complication was somewhat managed through the collection of data which measured the contribution of each corporation in the community. Fortson Conveyers, as a British firm, was not a complete weakness of this study because it has unique data that can be discussed in the section of corporate philosophy, which in turn adds to a deeper understanding of the cultural factors related to philanthropic activities. The third concern is the refusal of an interview by Kentucky Bluegrass United Way. Initially, there was an expectation that the organization would offer many insights into the relationship between the community and companies on philanthropy and the nature of philanthropic activities of Japanese companies in detail. However, an interview with the director was not possible, and therefore, perspectives of the recipient side were not comprehensive.

NOTES

1. All the names of the communities, the non-profit organizations and the corporations under investigation are pseudonyms.

2. The four experts are: Dr. Lorraine Garkovich (Professor of Community and Leadership Development, University of Kentucky); Dr. James G. Hougland Jr. (Professor of Sociology, University of Kentucky); Dr. Rick Maurer (Extension Professor of Community and Leadership Development, University of Kentucky); Dr. Ronald Hustedde (Professor of Community and Leadership Development, University of Kentucky).

Chapter Four

Research Setting—A Community

A HISTORIC OVERVIEW OF HEARTLAND

The city of Heartland is a thriving community in Kentucky's Bluegrass Region surrounded by beautiful horse farms. In 1999, a national magazine introduced Heartland as one of the successful small towns in America. Entering the downtown area, we can see that many buildings are occupied and that people have pleasant conversations with each other. By these indications, we can sense that, though it is small, this community is thriving.

Heartland is located within General County which had a population of 27,697 in 2000. Located 35 miles south of Lexington, Heartland has had a significant role in Kentucky history. Although not incorporated until 1836 (Brown, 1992), the city was actually founded in 1784 by Walker Daniel, the first district attorney of Kentucky (1783–84). At that time, Kentucky was a part of Virginia, and in the late 18th century, the legislature of Virginia decided to place a supreme court in the District of Kentucky, and housed it in the town square of Heartland. Ten conventions were held in Heartland, and in 1792, the first constitution of the Commonwealth of Kentucky was written.

The city's reputed excellent school system is one of the special features of Heartland that makes this community vibrant. Educated people have a significant role in community development. An executive director of the General County Community Development Council (GCCDC) mentions that:

There is a really strong sense of volunteering, of volunteerism here. There is a real strong sense of doing things right way. Even though they might have spent more money, or might take longer. There is a lot of good leadership here. Because of Middleway College and because of other historical trends and what not there, there is a large educated group in General County and Heartland and

43

that sees their sense of the future and want to get a part of it. So, it has been a blessing for any community to have a huge educated population that wants to be a part of the community. So, that's blessing.

This observation is supported by a study conducted by Hodgkinson et al. They found that religious involvement is highly correlated with giving and volunteering. Also, full-time employment status, higher education, marital status and household income have positive relationships with giving and volunteering (cited by Galper, 1999).

As mentioned by the executive director of the GCCDC, Middleway College has a very important role in the community. Rated as one of the nation's top 50 liberal arts colleges, with approximately 1,100 students undertaking its four-year program, its alumni include two U.S. vice presidents, one Chief Justice of the United States, 13 U.S. Senators, 44 U.S. Representatives and 11 governors. The alumni are also reputed to be leaders in the fields of teaching, medicine, business, law and journalism. The endowment per alumni is ranked number one among the nation's colleges and universities, and the school's connections outside the community, as well as its activities within the community, enhance the development of the community in turn. Ninety seven percent of the students live on campus, and the college encourages them to be active in community services, with around 60 percent of them participating in volunteer work in the community.

Another noted school in Heartland is a Kentucky School for the Deaf, the first publicly financed school of its kind. The other schools located in Heartland include Heartland Theological Seminary and The Institute for Young Ladies. Heartland's public schools are also highly regarded for their excellent programs and student achievement. For example, Heartland High School earned the distinguished recognition of being a National School of Excellence.

Historically, Heartland was developed as a commercial hub for railroad transportation, as the nation's railroads prospered in the 19th Century. However, in 1970, the passenger service from a Heartland depot ended, as automobiles became the preferred mode of transportation. It was also marked the end of the railroad system's role in Heartland's economic development. During the 19th Century, Heartland experienced sporadic industrial development as a commercial hub: some factories were built, but disappeared years later. In the early 20th Century, there was the possibility of both a feed and grain milling company and a suit and coat manufacturer, entering Heartland's economy. However, it was not until the 1960s that industry began to take an important role in the community (Brown, 1992).

During the 1960s, new industrial development emerged on the western and southern part of the city, largely due to the establishment of the General County

Industrial Foundation. This foundation got its start through the sale of 100,000 dollars in stock to individuals and businesses, including local banks. It held its first organizational meeting on May 16, 1962. The Industrial Foundation purchases under-utilized land, mainly from farmers, after which they installed utilities and sewers in order to build an industrial park. Finally, they sell a parcel of land to industries (Brown, 1992). The mission of the Industrial Foundation is to create industrial jobs by attracting industries into General County. To accomplish this mission, the Industrial Foundation closely works with city, county and state governments, as well as the Heartland-General County Chamber of Commerce. In fact, the Chamber of Commerce and the Industrial Foundation are housed on the same floor of a building in downtown Heartland. Over the years, the Industrial Foundation has become the gatekeeper for recruiting industries, setting a bar on what type of industries they will welcome. For instance, they felt that heavy industries, or those that would employ thousands of people, would be inappropriate for their community, due to the potential of pollution or economic dependency on a single company. Because of this strict requirement, in its early years, the Industrial Foundation was not able to attract the industries as they had hoped. However, after they later relaxed these requirements, General County began to attract industries. Also, their bargain price (one-half to two-thirds of market price) was appealing for the industries. During its 40 year history, the Industrial Foundation has been responsible for attracting 20 industries and 5,000 jobs into the county.

Viewmont Corporation first occupied the Industrial Foundation's industrial park in 1965. The company built a distribution center for greeting cards and other products, employing 800 people. In 1971, Preasant Corporation built a plant near the industrial park, which produced trash compacters and other products, employing approximately 1,000 people. Although it was outside the industrial park, the Industrial Foundation worked with the company by sharing information. Fortson Conveyers that manufactures conveyers and employs several hundred people moved into the park during the mid-1970s. Several other companies had also moved in during this time. In addition to the active role of the Industrial Foundation, the opening of a bypass accelerated the influx of industries into the western and southern part of the city (Brown, 1992).

THE INDUSTRIAL FOUNDATION AND INDUSTRIAL COUNCIL

A unique trait of Heartland is the active role industrial leaders play in community affairs. Although Middleway College has taken a leadership role in the community, industrial leaders also started to take a leadership role as the importance of the industrial sector increased in the community. Heartland has a subsidiary of the Industrial Foundation called the General County Industrial Council. This is a group of executives and human resources managers who represent Heartland's leading companies, along with representatives of Kentucky Utilities and Erickson McIntosh Regional Hospital. The meetings are held once a month at a restaurant, usually at lunch time. Although the council began as part of the Industrial Foundation, it has gained independence over time. Today, the role of the President of the Industrial Foundation has been reduced to that of participant only in the council's meetings.

The Industrial Council's meeting is closed door, but very informal affair, and what goes on behind its closed doors is never leaked to the outside world. This is probably the main reason why its participants feel free to discuss issues openly. They go around the table and share information that addresses issues such as the current state of business, whether they are hiring or laying off employees, if business is picking up or slowing down, and what the current salary level and staff turnover rate is, among others. They also discuss issues affecting the community. For example, there was an accident involving a train and a car, creating a fire with chemicals. On that day, it affected the community and businesses. They discussed how the community could prepare for future accidents like this.

Over the years, the Industrial Council has become quite influential in the community. It has created a norm that each industry has to consider neighboring industries, discouraging selfish corporate behaviors in the community. For example, when companies hire people, they set a wage level comparable to other neighboring companies. It is possible that a new company hires people by offering five dollars an hour more than the other existing companies, effectively stealing employees from other companies. After a time, if the company discovers they cannot maintain such wage levels, they are either forced to lower the wages or close down. The Industrial Council implicitly discourages this kind of corporate behavior. Also, when the city of Heartland attracts an industry through the Industrial Foundation, the Industrial Council evaluates whether the incoming company will conflict with the existing industries. In order to avoid competition among the companies in Heartland, they try to recruit a company that manufactures different products from the existing companies. The Industrial Council encourages cooperative relationship among industries and creates a sense of community, and co-existence and sustainability are the important guiding principles of its members.

This is in contrast to the neighboring city of Middletown, where there is no such organization. Despite the fact that many of the companies in

Middletown are located close to each other, they have little knowledge one another's operations. As a result, the industrial sector in Middletown does not take a community leadership role in the same way Heartland's industry does, where the Industrial Council can be seen as an embodiment of social capital, an important feature of vibrant community. Social capital refers to the features of social organization, such as trust, norms, and networks, which can improve the efficiency of society by facilitating coordinated actions (Putnam, 1993:167). The Industrial Council nurtures a norm where each firm thinks about other companies and its community with long-term perspectives when they make corporate decisions. It discourages corporate behaviors of short-term self-interest.

SOCIOECONOMIC OVERVIEW OF HEARTLAND

Looking at the socioeconomic indicators of the city, Heartland is a typical example of a small Kentucky community. In the year 2000, the total population in Heartland was 15,477 (as shown in Table 4.1). The populations for 1970, 1980 and 1990 were 11,542, 12,942 and 12,420, respectively. The population had increased between 1970 and 1980 by 12.13 percent, however, between 1980 and 1990, the population had decreased slightly by 4.03 percent. The population then grew rapidly between 1990 and 2000, with a 24.61 percent increase.

Among the population in 1990, 10,384 were white and 1,939 were African-American. Other races include 37 American Indians, 24 Japanese, 7 Koreans, 15 Samoans and 14 other minority groups. In the year 2000, the breakdown of the population was: 12,949 whites, 2,015 African-Americans, 38 American Indians, 128 Asians (Asian Indians 32, Chinese 12, Filipino 5, Japanese 46, Koreans 11, Vietnamese 2 and other Asians 20), 6 Native Hawaiians and other Pacific Islanders, and 127 other races. The white population had increased between 1990 and 2000 by 24.7 percent. However, the African-Americans' growth rate was small, at just 3.91 percent between 1990 and 2000. Although the numbers were small, the growth of Asians and other

Table 4.1. Population and Population Change, Heartland, KY

Pop. 1970	Pop. 1980	Pop. 1990	Pop. 2000	Percent Change 70–80	Percent Change 80–90	Percent Change 90–2000
11,542	12,942	12,420	15,477	12.13	-4.03	24.61

(U.S. Bureau of the Census, Census 2000)

Table 4.2. Population and Population Change by Race, Heartland, KY

Race	Pop. 1990	Pop. 2000	Percent Change 1990–2000
White	10,384	12,949	24.7
African-American	1,939	2,015	3.91
American Indians	37	38	0.03
Asians	31	128	312.9
(Japanese)	(24)	(46)	(91.7)
Hawaiians & Pacific Islanders	15	6	−60
Others	14	127	807.14

(U.S. Census Bureau, Census 1990 and 2000)

races was noteworthy (as shown in Table 4.2), increasing by 312.9 percent, and other races increased by 807.14 percent between 1990 and 2000. Thus, Heartland has become a more diverse population. The Japanese population almost doubled during the decade.

Educational attainment in Heartland was slightly better than the state's educational attainment. In 2000, among persons 25 years and over in Heartland, 21.8 percent had education less than high school (as shown in Table 4.3). On the other hand, in 2000, among persons 25 years and over in Kentucky, 25.9 percent had education less than high school. In Heartland, 78.2 percent of the person 25 years and over completed high school. The state's average high school completion rate was 74.1 percent. Also, 22.7 percent of the persons 25 years and over in Heartland had bachelor's and graduate/professional degrees. On the other hand, 17.1 percent of the age group had those degrees in the state.

The total labor force in Heartland was 5,356 in 1990, with an unemployment rate of 8.6 percent, or approximately 460 people. Although not Heartland-Specific, the data on unemployment figures for the entire General County area indicates there was a decline of the unemployment rate to 4.1 percent in 1997, with a further decline to 3.0 percent by July 1998. In the

Table 4.3. Educational Attainment in Heartland and Kentucky, 2000

	Heartland	Kentucky
Education Less than High School	21.8 percent	25.9 percent
High School Completion Rate for the Persons 25 year and Older	78.2 percent	74.1 percent
Percent of People Who Hold Bachelor's and Graduate/Professional Degrees	22.7 percent	17.1 percent

(U.S. Bureau of the Census, Census 2000)

Census 2000, Heartland's labor force had risen to 7,259, and the unemployment rate was only 2.7 percent. Manufacturing industry is partly responsible for this decrease in unemployment. In the 1990s, 11 manufacturing companies moved into Heartland, inclusive of one company that took over the operations of a factory that was likely to shut down. These 11 companies created 2,269 jobs collectively.

Median household income in Heartland was US$21,119 in 1989, increasing to $32,937 in 1999. This was lower than the state's median family income of $22,534 in 1989 and $33,672 in 1999. In 1989, 20 percent of the population in Heartland was under the poverty level, and in 1999, this shrank to 12.4 percent. Though Heartland is better off in terms of the decrease of poverty incidence, the trend was similar to the state's poverty level from 19 percent (1989) to 15.8 percent (1999).

Regarding the community's transport systems, Heartland is serviced by U.S. Highways 127 and 150. The Norfolk Southern Corporation has a railroad system which runs through the city. The Blue Grass Airport in Lexington is 38 miles north of Heartland.

THE MANUFACTURING SECTOR IN HEARTLAND

Manufacturing companies in Heartland have a significant role in its economy, with 22 industrial establishments in operation. Most of them are located in industrial parks, many of which belong to either the Industrial Foundation or are managed by private corporations. The manufacturing companies are in an open space, yet are close to downtown. Most of the 22 companies are American, such as B. B. Fishwater & Sons Company, Goodman Track Components, Dancing Corporation and Blue Wing Shoe Company.

B. B. Fishwater & Sons Company is the second largest employer in Heartland, employing 1,100 people. Located in an industrial park on the east side of the city, it is a branch plant whose headquarters is in Chicago. B. B. Fishwater is in a printing business with $5.42 billion sales and 34,000 employees worldwide. In its Heartland plant, it produces magazines such as Seventeen, Vanity Fair and the New Yorker Magazine etc. The operation in Heartland started in 1985, and since then it has been an important player in the community.

Goodman Track Components is a new comer to the Heartland community. It started in 1997 and the facility was opened in the fall of 1998. The company is a part of Goodman Incorporated, the headquarters of which is located in Illinois. Goodman Track Components employs about 100 people, and produces track pins and bushing solely for Goodman's clickety-clack type vehicles. Its parent company, Goodman Incorporated, has $24 billion in sales and 66,000 employees worldwide. Although the operation in Heartland is small, it has been very active within the community since its establishment.

Fortson Conveyer was acquired by the British corporation FKI-PLC in 1987. Initially, the company moved to Heartland from Pennsylvania between 1974 and 1976, when it was owned by an American company called Rexnord Company. Along with its two other branch facilities in Ohio and Canada, Fortson Conveyer produces conveyers, sortation devices, and automatic transfer cars, employing about 300 people in its Heartland branch alone. Although British capital limits its activities, it has been very active in the community.

Heartland has three Japanese companies, all of which are located in industrial parks in the west part of the city. Their presence is important in the city. In 1999, there were 5,594 people employed by all the manufacturing companies in Heartland, including American and Japanese owned. Among those, Japanese companies employed 2,601 people (46.5% of the total manufacturing sector employment in Heartland).

Kagoshima Home Appliance Corporation of America employs 1,700 people, and is the biggest employer in General County. It is the largest producer of vacuum cleaners and microwave ovens in North America, with its products being exported under the brand names Panaplex and OEM to the Middle East, Africa and Australia. Kagoshima initially entered into a joint venture with the vacuum cleaner division of the Whirlpool Company, but in 1990, obtained 100% share of the company. As a result, the location of Kagoshima's plant was not a careful consideration on their behalf; however, a Kagoshima executive said that Heartland has an excellent labor force. People in this area do not relocate as often as those living in Los Angeles and New York, and this enhances the stability that is so important in factory operations. A relatively safe environment and beautiful landscape are very attractive for Japanese people working here, and safety is one of primary concerns for the Japanese.

Located across the road from Kagoshima is another Japanese company, the Dainichi Manufacturing Corporation, which produces generators, compressors and welders for industrial use. A small company, Dainichi employs 50 people, of which 5 are Japanese and 45 are American. The company came to Kentucky for several reasons, the most important reason of which was the appreciation of the yen against the dollar. Dainichi had exported products to the United States for many years, however, the appreciation of the yen in the late 1980s made these exports uneconomical. After an American company selling Dainichi products in the United States asked Dainichi to produce the products in the United States, another option for Dainichi appeared. At the same time, a representative office of Kentucky in Japan was aggressive in attracting Dainichi to the state, and its incentive package was a critical factor in its appeal. Another factor was a good labor force in this area. The people were also perceived as warm and friendly, and the city was reputed to be relatively safe. The company viewed Heartland as a good location to do business, and to date they are satisfied with the location.

GTS Wire and Cable is the oldest Japanese company operating in Heartland, having bought a similar operation from the Firestone Company in February 1981. It produces steel cords for automobile tires and the hose wires usually used in gasoline station pumps. As of 2000, the company employs 674 people, including six expatriates from Japan. GTS Wire and Cable is a subsidiary of Yokohama Rope Manufacturing Company Ltd., which has its headquarters in Tokyo and employs about 3,000 people. GTS's major customers are tire makers in the United States, including Goodyear and General Tire. Because it is the oldest Japanese company in Heartland, the relationship between GTS, local governments and other neighboring industries has been well established.

Although Heartland is attractive, most Japanese choose to live in Lexington, 38 miles northeast of the city, and commute to Heartland every day. For Japanese singles or business bachelors, Heartland does not offer much in the way of leisure, being a 'dry' county. Usually Japanese workers like to go to bars after work, but the city does not offer this service. Also, since they do no have wives who cook Japanese food for them, they are likely to eat out, and as such, Japanese restaurants are necessary for them. Japanese restaurants offer their favorite Japanese meals and alcohol such as *sake*. For example, one of the Japanese business bachelors, who works in a city located about 35 miles south of Lexington, visits a Japanese restaurant almost everyday for dinner and drinks. Japanese families also prefer to stay in Lexington, mainly because it offers better schools and cultural events. In addition, a Japanese Saturday school is offered in Lexington for elementary and middle school students. Since they will go back to Japan after several years of assignment, their life plan is targeted to how well they can readjust to life back in Japan after the assignment in the United States is over. The Saturday school is very important to keep up with the Japanese educational standard, which culminates in extremely difficult examinations for entrance into Japan's universities. Lexington is very convenient for Japanese wives, too, with its Japanese grocery stores that sell Japanese food and rent videos of Japanese TV series. The availability of Japanese food is an important factor to choosing to stay in Lexington.

As a place to live, Heartland does not offer things Japanese want. However, it is a very good place to do business, and the interaction between local & state governments and Japanese companies is very smooth. In particular, cooperation between the groups has enabled the amicable settlement of any problems. When the companies ask for something, the local and state govern ments are quick to respond. For example, when the economy rapidly grew in the 1990s, the low unemployment figures made it difficult for the companies to sustain quality employees. After the Japanese companies complained to the state government about this situation, the government immediately began to try and find ways to resolve the issue which is resulting from the low un employment figures, despite challenges involved in solving such a problem (Yotsumoto, 2001).

KENTUCKY BLUEGRASS UNITED WAY

Kentucky Bluegrass United Way in Heartland is an active organization work ing for human and community needs. Nestled between a row of small, inex pensive and deteriorating houses on its left, and a huge building which houses Erickson McIntosh Regional Hospital on the right, the Kentucky Bluegrass United Way is located in a downtown neighborhood that is a contrast between rundown and modern structures. The United Way's building itself is small and old, with a sign out front that reads: "COMMUNITY HOUSE." Shared with the American Red Cross, it is a center of community care activities in Heartland. Upon entering the building, it is easy to see that the center's op erational costs are low: an old couch, such as one might find in the Goodwill or Salvation Army, can be found, along with office rooms with no doors, and a small kitchen. The building itself, in fact, gives little indication of the scale of the operation, but the new computers do. Kentucky Bluegrass United Way in Heartland covers Central Kentucky areas for its services, and its mission is "to increase the organized capacity of people to care for one another."

The United Way is a highly visible charity organization, established in the United States in 1887. Hundreds of thousands of Americans have joined its causes by volunteering and/or donating money at work sites, making it Amer ica's largest federated charity organization, with more than 2,200 local United Ways throughout the United States. The United Way's ability to raise a large amount of money, as well as how it raises that money, makes this organization very powerful in the voluntary sector. Basically each local organization has three functions to fulfill: coordination and planning for community needs, fund raising, and the distribution, or allocation, of funds raised (Brilliant, 1990).

Heartland's gifts to the United Way are way above average when compared to other communities of similar population. For its 1999 campaign, the United Way in General County[1] collected a total of US$1,046,147 (as shown in Table 4.4). The amount is striking compared to other five comparable communities

Table 4.4. Kentucky Bluegrass United Way 1999 Campaign Statistics Compared to Other Comparable Sized Communities

Community	Pop.	Campaign Total Dollar	Dollar Raised Per Capita	# of Emp.	Dollar Raised Per Person Employed	5 Year % Increase	10 Year % Increase
General County (Heartland), Kentucky	27700	1046147	37.77	13859	75.49	96.5	339.6
Ludington, Michigan	27900	367034	13.16	13803	26.59	59.6	103.9
Ponca City, Oklahoma	27807	644471	23.18	12552	51.34	14.5	-1.7
Wytheville, Virginia	26700	174519	6.54	14460	12.07	NA	66.8
Berwick, Pennsylvania	25628	342294	13.36	12258	27.92	55.6	34
Kenton, Ohio	25600	129180	5.05	12054	10.72	14.3	52

(Created from United Way of America, 1999-2000 Leaderboard Summary, 2000)

mentioned here. The entire area of General County where Heartland exists had a population of 27,700 in 1999. They raised more than one million dollars. This means that each person in General County donated $37.77 to the United Way. In comparison, the city of Ludington in Michigan, which had a population of 27,900 in 1999, raised $367,034 for its 1999 campaign, or $13.16 dollars per capita. Ponca City, Oklahoma, with a population of 27,807 in 1999, raised $644,471 in its 1999 campaign, or $23.18 per person. Wytheville, Virginia, with a population of 26,700 in 1999, raised $ 174,519 for its 1999 United Way campaign, or $6.54 per person. Berwick, Pennsylvania, with a population of 25,628 in 1999, raised $342,294 in the same year, or $13.36 per person. Finally, Kenton, Ohio, with a population of 25,600 in 1999, raised $129,180, or $5.05 per capita. There are many places in which multimillion dollars are donated to the United Way, but these communities can be considered as outliers. These outliers occur when one time donations by individuals are made, or in communities in which CEOs of big corporations live and donate. When we exclude these outliers, and compare similar communities, the result of the United Way campaign in General County is exceptional, and is supported by a wide spectrum of citizens.

All of these six communities had a similar level of employment. For example, in 1999 Ludington had an employment of 13,803, while General County had an employment of 13,859. Among these six communities, the smallest number of employees was 12,054 in Kenton, while the largest number was in Wytheville, with 14,460. When looking at the dollar raised per person employed, General County is exceptional. In 1999, the County raised $75.49 per person employed, while Ludington raised $26.59, Ponca City $51.34, Wytheville $12.07, Berwick $27.92 and Kenton raised $10.72 per employee. This means that General County in which the city of Heartland resides raised seven times as much money for the United Way as Kenton did.

Kentucky Bluegrass United Way in Heartland has not always been a strong federated charity organization. They have had a 96.5 percent increase in the past 5 years, and in terms of a ten year span, equates to a 339.6 percent increase. Five years ago, the United Way in Heartland raised $532,390, and $241,070 ten years ago. Compared to the United Way in Heartland, Ponca City had a 14.5 percent increase in the last five years, but in its ten year span, actually decreased by 1.7 percent. This means that the United Way in Ponca City raised $562,856 in 1994, and $655,616 in 1989. In 1989, Berwick raised $219,983, and in 1994, it raised $255,443, which equates to a 55.6 percent increase in five years and a 34.0 percent increase over ten years. As these figures indicate, General County's fundraising efforts for the United Way campaign have been phenomenal, but its growth has been significant in only the last 10 years.

Money raised by Kentucky Bluegrass United Way is used for six major objectives, which all center around the improvement of people's quality of life and their community. These objectives are: preventing violence & crime, providing basic needs, supporting education & literacy, empowering seniors, strengthening families & children, and building youth & community leadership. These objectives are pursued by providing support to twenty three agencies. Table 4.5 shows how the United Way's money was allocated.

Table 4.5. A List of Agencies Supported by Kentucky Bluegrass United Way and Amount of Money Supported, 1999

Names of Agencies	What They Do	Money Allocated (USD)
American Red Cross Central Kentucky Chapter	Provides disaster relief and community education for emergency awareness.	34,000
Bluegrass Rape Crisis Center	Provide support and information to victims of rape and/or sexual assault and to their families and friends.	6,920
Central Kentucky Legal Services	Provides civil legal assistance to low-income people.	6,000
Vocational Industrial Service	Helps people with a physical, emotional, or mental disability to become employed.	27,000
The Recovery Center	Provides individual and family outpatient treatment for drug abuse/dependence and domestic violence.	18,000
YWCA Spouse Abuse Center	Offers crisis intervention and shelter to victims of domestic violence and their families.	12,389
Blue Grass Community Action Self-Sufficiency Program	Helps low-income families become self-sufficient by offering career counseling, training, affordable child care, transportation, and clothing.	3,000
Family Services Association	Offers financial help to families in an emergency situation.	29,000
Heartland/General County Literacy Council	Teaches adults how to read and write through one-on-one instruction. Also, English is offered for speakers of other languages.	12,000
Salvation Army	Provides food, clothing, shelter, and utilities to people in emergency situations. Offers character building, educational, recreational and life skills programs for children, youth and adults.	94,000

(continued)

Table 4.5.   (*continued*)

Names of Agencies	What They Do	Money Allocated (USD)
Urban League	Provides training for low-income adults which leads to employment opportunities.	30,000
The Crisis Stabilization Cottage	Provides short term emergency crisis stabilization for children and youth, ages 6 to 18, and counseling for their families.	20,000
Blue Grass Community Action Senior Companion Program	Serves home-bound elderly people by providing companions who assist with transportation, light housekeeping, and respite for caregivers.	8,500
Senior Citizens Center	Provides home care, personal care, information, and referral services for the elderly.	66,000
Hospice	Provides in-home skilled nursing care in the late 6 months of terminal illness.	3,500
Nursing Home Ombudsman Agency	Helps nursing home resident express concerns, assert legal rights, and maintain dignity.	10,000
4-H Council	Offers programs designed to help young people learn and develop life skills.	12,500
Big Brothers / Big Sisters	Provides personal relationships between a child of a single-parent and an adult volunteer.	20,000
Blue Grass Council Boy Scouts of America	Provides programs for youth to develop self-esteem and leadership ability.	14,850
Heartland Learning Disabilities Association	Provides support and advocacy for children and families with learning disabilities.	5,000
Girl Scouts	Provides programs for girls ages 5 to 17 to develop high values, self-esteem and leadership qualities, and explore career opportunities.	14,500
Child Development Center	Provides evaluation, training, and therapy for preschool children with mental or physical disabilities.	60,000
YMCA	Provides programs to promote and develop wholesome lifestyles.	41,500
Special Allocations	This is for agencies which seek short-term financial aid when a lack of funding limits or threatens to eliminate critical community services.	172,000

(Kentucky Bluegrass United Way, 2000)

Some of the agencies in the list have a strong connection with the United Way historically. The Boy Scouts, Salvation Army, YMCA, Red Cross, YWCA, and Girl Scouts are agencies which the United Way supports nationwide, its relationships dating back as far as the 1930s. Over the years, the United Way's nationwide contribution to various agencies has changed (Brilliant, 1990), with agencies in arts, culture and civic activities obtaining more funds. In 1970, 5.3 percent of United Way funds were allocated to arts and culture, while 8.1 percent went to civic activities. In the same year, 38.6 percent of the funding went to health and welfare. In contrast, in 1985, arts and culture activities were supported by 11.1 percent of the United Way's funds, and civic activities were supported by 16.5 percent. In the same year, only 29.2 percent of the funds went to health and welfare activities. These figures indicate that the United Way reaches out nationwide to a great variety of people and community needs more than before. Nevertheless, many community leaders still believe that the United Way is a primary care unit for people's health and welfare in their community.

The belief in the United Way as a primary care organization in the community has been created by citizens' attachment to the community, as well as the United Way's effort to be an efficient organization. In other words, the first reason is an idealistic explanation and the second one is a rational one. American mentality cannot be separated from the notion of community, as it is a central belief for many Americans that it is a place for mutual support and belonging. Some communities try to present such an image as reality, and this longing for community synchronizes with the belief in the United Way system: supporting the United Way means nurturing the community in which they reside. Brilliant says that:

> *For many Americans, the United Way has become a symbol of volunteerism, based on its perceived attachment to basic values of community, workplace, charity, and business. Ever since the days of the community chest in the 1930s federated fund-raising organizations appear to have consciously cultivated their connection to fundamental American beliefs, deliberately building on the notion that they represent a "movement" in support of Americanism. Indeed, United Way has consistently helped to promote a myth of organized charity as linked to the very heart of American community life (Brilliant, 10).*

Corporations and workers believe in the United Way as an organization for people and community. This belief helps to maintain and perpetuate the relationship among the United Way, corporations and community.

In recent years, there have been challenges to the United Way system from various organizations (e.g., Black United Funds and Social Action Funds) that seek access to the workplace for donations. They are voices that are not

heard in the United Way system of raising and distributing money, and it is a
challenge to the domination of charity by the majority which tends to exclude
the voices of minority groups. Although they have gained access to charitable
activities in local communities, many of those communities still keep the
United Way as a primary federated charity organization. This is also true for
Heartland, where Kentucky Bluegrass United Way has a very large presence
in the community, and is the largest charity organization in Heartland. Almost
all corporations, especially in the industrial sector, donate money primarily
to the United Way, after which they usually donate money to a second and/or
third charity organization of their choice.

The United Way's effort to be an efficient charitable organization is also
a primary reason corporations want to support it, with its efficiency in getting maximum dollars to those in need being more than well known among
business leaders: it has become legendary (Conference Board, Berman). A
corporate leader whom the author interviewed in Heartland said: "They (the
United Way) have an incredibly low overhead rate. They are demanding and
tell agencies that ask for money what they have to do to get their money." Its
performance is another reason that corporations believe in the United Way
system, and observation of the United Way office in Heartland attests to its
low overhead rate. As described, the office is thrifty, with minimal, but functional, equipment.

Another reason that many corporations want to support the United Way
is the wide range of organizations which it funds. As shown previously,
Kentucky Bluegrass United Way funds two dozen agencies, representing
different areas of human need, and supporting people and community in a
more comprehensive way than any other single agency. In communities,
company employees are also beneficiaries of services provided by the United
Way funded agencies. Employees have different needs and, of course, their
company wants to support its employees rather than unknown people. When
the company donates money to the United Way, it has more of a chance to
serve its employees through the agencies. This is also true geographically. Although many companies employ people from Heartland, there are also a large
number of commuters. For example, Goodman Track Components employs
people from 18 surrounding counties, most of them from a five county area,
with only a few employees actually living in Heartland. The United Way's
comprehensive and multi-county services meet the needs of the corporation,
so by supporting Kentucky Bluegrass United Way, services are provided to
the largest number of their employees.

The United Way's popularity, as well as generality in providing services,
has a lot of appeal to corporations. Because it is a national organization
with more than 2,200 local organizations, it is convenient for a corporate

headquarters to deal with it. Wherever a company locates branch offices and factories, the community has a local United Way, with each local branch having a similar range of agencies to fund. This means that when a company with many different locations decides to support the United Way, it can easily establish a corporate wide philanthropic guideline or policy. In addition, its charitable expenses can be less controversial, making funding approval easier. For many large corporations, the United Way is the only federated charity organization that is allowed to access the workplace for donations. In Heartland, for example, Kagoshima allows only Kentucky Bluegrass United Way to access its work site for a campaign. Also, for B. B. Fishwater's local contribution fund, the United Way is the only federated charity organization. In essence, what we see in Heartland is a very strong relationship between the United Way and corporations that have facilities there.

NOTE

1. For Heartland, County level data was used in order to compare with other communities which have similar level of population and employment.

Chapter Five

Human Resource Management and Corporate Social Responsibility

HUMAN RESOURCE MANAGEMENT

Since the late 1980s, many Japanese firms have built factories in Kentucky. By 2004, there were 137 companies operating in the state, employing 34,256 people (Kentucky Cabinet for Economic Development, 2004). The form of Japanese direct investment to Kentucky has been to establish manufacturing facilities, especially in auto-related industries. Kentucky has attracted Japanese auto-related industries because it is one of the "auto corridor" states, where 70 percent of the auto plants in the U.S. are located (Klier and Johnson, 2000). The proximity between assembly plants and parts suppliers is an important factor for the efficient implementation of the Just-in-Time production system. Toyota's first US assembly plant,[1] established in Kentucky in 1986, brought many associated supplier firms with it. The state and local governments have provided incentive packages to these firms. Many of these firms struggle to establish themselves as a solid company financially and socially on American soil. Japanese manufacturing firms in the U.S. have had many successful and unsuccessful experiences in transplanting their management styles, including team work and total quality management, and human resource management is one area in which the Japanese have a different practice from American business management.

Pucik and Hatvany (1983) identify three human resource management strategies in Japanese firms.[2] First, they emphasize on the internal labor market. When a position is vacant, they look for candidates from within the organization. They also have the practices of job rotation and long-term employment. Second, they have a company philosophy that expresses concerns for employees. This philosophy creates many fringe benefits, such as subsidizing health insurance, commuting costs and housing, and the gap between white-collar and blue-collar workers is small in these benefits. Third, they focus on cooperation and teamwork. They practice team-based employee activities and consensus-style decision making. The emphasis on these qualities nurtures employees who are loyal to the company, and develops a shared responsibility to the company products.[3]

Not all subsidiaries of Japanese corporations in the United States are willing to transfer Japanese management to their facilities in the United States, depending rather on their environment.[4] The environment for Japanese companies differs by industry types and the location of the facility. One of the differences in the environment between Japan and the United States is the local labor market, and the understanding of this market has been identified as an important part of business success.[5]

In the United States, the labor market is more developed and mobile, especially in large cities. Because Japanese management, especially human resource management, requires a relatively stable labor force, the transfer of Japanese internal labor market practices and human capital investment is influenced by a labor market condition of the area (Pfeffer, 1983). Six Japanese auto makers in the auto corridor chose communities that have few minorities and abundant young workers, along with minimal union activity (Perrucci, 1994). Kentucky's labor force is also considered to be a good choice for Japanese manufacturing firms because it is relatively stable, having little experience in union activities (Karan and Bladen, 2001).[6]

RECRUITMENT AND RETENTION AS FACTORS INFLUENCING CORPORATE ATTITUDES ON GIVING

In recent years, for firms to be competitive, there has been a shift in emphasis from physical resources (e.g., product & process technology and access to financial markets) to human resources (Greening and Turban 2000). A company's main source of success has been gradually recognized as how well the firm selects and manages a quality workforce, and recruiting and retaining a good workforce has become a key factor for a company's success in its business operations. There is a body of literature that studies the relationships between group identity and recruitment and retention of workers. Usually, these studies use social identity theory as their guide. Social identity is defined as "that part of an individual's self-concept which derives from his knowledge of his membership in a social group (or groups) together with the value and emotional significance attached to that membership" (Tajfel, 1978:63). The membership in a group becomes both positive and negative for the development of one's self-image. In the context of recruitment, it is reasoned that a firm identified as attractive is more likely to receive applications than an unattractive firm. In considering the context of retention, an attractive firm can retain their workers better than an unat-tractive firm (Abrams et al. 1998). As mentioned in the literature review chapter, Scott (1995) talks about cognitive structure in institutional theory. Such structure allows organizational actors and/or individual actors to de-fine themselves as who they are and act accordingly. The social identity theory is a way of comprehending the cognitive structure in institutions, and has contributed to understanding the behavioral patterns of employees. When employees are happy with their workplace, they are more likely to stay with the company (Abrams et al. 1998).

One of the ways that the company can make its organization attrac-tive is to be active in corporate citizenship. Greening and Turban (2000) studied this issue by examining the relationship between corporate social performances and attracting quality workforce, using the social identity and signaling theories to conceptualize the relationship. The signaling theory suggests that job applicants can interpret the working conditions of a com-pany by analyzing the signals sent by the organization, media, friends, and communities. They reasoned that potential applicants receive information about a firm's corporate social performance as signals and interpret it. The interpretation becomes a basis for the perception of working conditions. The perception determines the attractiveness of the company for the poten-tial applicants. The result of this study shows that companies scoring higher in corporate social performance are perceived as more attractive employers than the companies that rank lower in corporate social performance. The more attractive a company is, the higher the probability that a job within its ranks will be pursued, culminating in the acceptance of a job offer after the interview process. An aspect of the Greening and Turban study that reduces its relevancy for this current study is the dimensions of corporate social performance construct. The construct is made up of four dimensions: 1) employee relations; 2) concern for the environment; 3) product quality; and 4) treatment of women and minorities. Community relations were dropped from the construct because it was not statistically significant. However, the researchers discuss their decision not to include it in the construct as a potential weakness in the study. They discovered this potential weak-ness by conducting two focus groups with university students, about why community relations were not perceived as important as other dimensions. As students typically have little experience with community relations or community projects, community relations are not considered an important factor for company attractiveness. If the researchers had chosen a different population, for example a population of real job seekers, the result might have been different, and possibly could have included community relations as a dimension of corporate social performance.

Some of the corporations in Heartland are aware of the relationship between corporate social performance and their attractiveness as a company, and use corporate philanthropic activities as a tool to be more appealing. This is in contrast to one of the Japanese firms in Heartland that has had problems with a high turnover rate. The company does not see the connection between corporate social responsibility, and their attractiveness as a firm for recruitment and retention of its workers.

Does active involvement in corporate citizenship benefit the corporation? If a company says "Yes" to this question, they are willing to contribute to the community. If a company says "No" to this question, they will be reluctant to participate in philanthropy. In this study, there are differences in understanding the relationship between corporate contribution and the benefit to the company among the corporations interviewed. This difference is important because it influences corporate behavior on philanthropy. Corporations which say "Yes" to the question often mentioned the benefits to the company in terms of recruitment and retention of workers. Active engagement in corporate philanthropy presents a positive image to potential workers and current employees, and helps them to feel good about where they work. Therefore, corporate philanthropy helps to retain employees and to recruit better workers. This study reveals that the understanding of the relationship between corporate giving and recruitment and retention is determined by the national origin of the company's ownership.

American Firms

The American companies of Goodman and B. B. Fishwater understand the relationship between corporate philanthropy and the recruitment & retention of workers, and therefore are willing to commit to community affairs. In response to a question about the benefit of involvement in the community, a manager at B. B. Fishwater states:

> *The question is absolutely [yes]. I mean this has been a major component of our magazine business. If we weren't well liked or respected in the community, we would not get employees to come and work here . . . But people recognize what we do here. People recognize we are good givers to the community . . . You know, we turnover about 20 percent of our employees every year. So, roughly 200 people every year at material handler level, maybe entry level, so we still get people to come here. They won't come here if this wasn't a good decent place*

to work. So, that's why community development indirectly benefits the business.
We have a good name, we do a lot of good things for the community, in turn, they
come and put in the good days of work. We are able to produce products.

This comment shows a clear indication of their understanding of the relationship between corporate philanthropy and recruitment.

In the case of Goodman, their comment does not explicitly mention the relationship between corporate giving and human resource management. This is because Goodman offers good wages and benefits. Their working environment is good, so employees do not quit so easily. Therefore, they do not have as many problems in recruitment and retention. But the following comment suggests the level of their commitment to the community. As will be mentioned in a chapter later, Goodman is the number one American donor to the United Way. A manager at Goodman states:

I think we want to be perceived as the substantial player in the community, and
not a silent part of it. We want to take an active role. We want to concern about
the living standard in the community and providing opportunities for people,
the majority of people and to primarily, there is an education . . . to support
young people. I think we want people to think this is a better place because the
Goodman is here. And as far as our facility, we wanna be seen as the special
place to work.

American corporations in Heartland are aware of the relationship between corporate social performance and their attractiveness as a company, and use corporate philanthropic activities as a tool to be more appealing. They practice strategic philanthropy that integrates philanthropy into the overall strategic planning of the corporation (Marx, 1998: 34), becoming a scheme to advance corporation's business objectives. This is in contrast with a Japanese firm in Heartland that has had problems with a high turnover rate. Despite the problem, the company does not see the connection between corporate social responsibility and their attractiveness as a firm for the recruitment and retention of its workers.

A British Firm

In Heartland, American corporations seem to understand the benefit of corporate philanthropy relating to their own businesses, but this is not necessarily the case for Fortson Conveyer (British company), which see the relationship between corporate giving and benefits for their business somewhat differently. The British company sees its role as a generator of profits for its shareholders, which is in line with the ideas of Friedman (1971), who advocated profit maximization as the sole goal of business. In the case of Fortson, the parent company in Britain does not want to spend money on the community, and Fortson is prohibited from donating to community agencies. They cannot give even a penny to charity. Essentially, the parent company's philosophy is that "there are shareholders and give the money to shareholders and let them give to the charities of their choice. We do not give their money to charities (a comment by a CEO at Fortson)." The importance of shareholders over community might reflect more of a national culture rather than a company philosophy. Currently, Fortson is owned by a British company called FKI-PLC, their predecessors also being a British company known as Bapkaki Industries. Both companies have similar policies on corporate giving; they do not want to give money to the community. This is not unusual for British firms. In Britain, philanthropy is not well accepted because it implies Victorian "do-gooderism." People think of it as elitist, patronizing, morally judgmental, and ineffective (Wright, 2001: 400).[7] The British culture influences Fortson's corporate philosophy regarding philanthropy.

Japanese Firms

Many Japanese firms do not fully understand what corporate philanthropy is all about because the government is expected to provide social welfare. In Japan, the government was viewed as the parent of the people and society in a quasi family (Nosco, 2002). This view has not disappeared in Japan, and occasionally it surfaces in various discourses. This is an influence of Confucian ideology that asks rulers to take benevolent action to their subjects in exchange for loyalty (Hendry, 1995). Although it is changing gradually, the social welfare safety nets still remain within the realm of government responsibility (London, 1991). Japanese corporations provided social support mostly to their employees as a form of adequate salary and subsidies in housing, recreation, etc., but not to people in wider communities.[8] Japanese corporations in Heartland come from this kind of social environment.

Generally, Japanese companies do not see the relationship between corporate giving and the benefit to their businesses, with the exception of Kagoshima. It has a large operation and knows American culture well, due to their long presence in the United States.

GTS modestly contributes to the community. However, the company does not perceive the relationship between corporate giving and recruitment and retention of workers clearly. GTS acknowledges that the participation in community improvement activities has benefits to the company, because the community recognizes and remembers the company name, which allows employees to feel confident when people know about their company.

However, they do not recognize corporate giving as a tool for recruitment & retention of workers, categorizing corporate giving as a different organizational matter from the management of human resources. One wonders if this is a factor in this firm's high rate of turnover. In Japan, around ten workers quit their job each year at a comparable GTS factory. However, at the Heartland plant, about ten workers quit their job each month, making the turnover rate in the Heartland plant 12 times higher than a comparable plant in Japan, a difference that is attributed to culture. Because this is a big problem for GTS, their primary emphasis is on securing employees. Therefore, they do not think that corporate giving and philanthropy are important concerns for doing business, and do not perceive the link between corporate giving and their recruitment and retention of workers. Instead, they wonder why an American tradition of corporate philanthropy is what it is. A manager states that "in Japan, people wonder why they have to donate money to charity when the company lays off their employees and cut salaries while restructuring the company. But, here in America, it is a natural cause to make donations. It seems money is donated to charity even during a period of lay offs (a comment by a GTS manager)." Their motivation to donate money to the community is not based on an understanding of the benefit. It comes from a norm which states that the community expects this from their corporation, and Japanese tend to follow the norms (Abrams 1998). In other words, GTS's corporate giving action operates in the realm of the normative structure of the institution.

In Dainichi, they see a conflict between employee welfare and corporate giving. It is conceived as a zero sum game, that is, when money is spent on corporate giving, they think it is at the expense of employee welfare. This is similar to the philosophy of GTS. A plant manager at Dainichi says that "the first thing we have to do is to benefit employees. It wouldn't do us any good if we pronounce that we have given a lot of money to some kind of organizations but you don't get a raise. You know, so we have asked, the first thing you have to take care is of your employees." At Dainichi, the first priority is the shareholders and employees. The community therefore becomes a secondary importance, and corporate giving is not a critical part of their business. The company thinks corporate philanthropy does not directly benefit the company, but admits that, indirectly, it will help to maintain a smooth relationship with the community. However, it is not essential to participate in corporate philanthropy to maintain a healthy community relationship. Dainichi reluctantly participates in corporate philanthropy because they feel it is a part of the American culture and the American way of business. Since they have a corporate philosophy like this, Dainichi does not believe it is necessary for the community to know what contributions they have made to the community. As a corporation, they do not see the connection between corporate giving and the recruitment and retention of workers. Compared to other leading Japanese companies like Toyota, Dainichi is a newcomer to the United States. The company does not have enough experience, nor practical knowledge, about its host country. Dainichi is a typical corporation in Japan, and as usual for Japanese companies, they compare the actions of other companies in the area to theirs, in order to decide what kind of corporate philosophy they need to embrace.[9]

Compared to GTS and Dainichi, Kagoshima has a more mature corporate philosophy on corporate giving in the U.S. The corporate identity of Kagoshima has been the same since the founding of Kagoshima by Konosuke Kagoshima. A Kagoshima manager states its corporate identity as:

> *Basically, because this is a manufacturing company, through products, basically through products, we will contribute to the society. New products and convenient products continue to generate new values. Through those products which we deliver to the society with fair prices, we will contribute to people's lives and the development of culture. This is our corporate philosophy since its founding.*

Kagoshima produces reliable products which consumers find acceptable. Electronic products made by Kagoshima have been trusted by Japanese as one of the most reliable products in Japan. However, in recent years, Kagoshima's reputation as an attractive company to new college & university graduates has decreased. As an example, Sony is the overall number one company in which new graduates of college & university students desire to work. On the other hand, Kagoshima ranked number eight (Diamond Big Company, 2001). Although Kagoshima produces reliable products and has an excellent reputation, it is perceived as lacking the creativity and/or new ideas one can find in a firm such as Sony.

Therefore, Kagoshima has contemplated how to improve its reputation, and in this context, is hoping that its activities in corporate philanthropy will help to improve its image. A Kagoshima manager mentions these benefits of involvement in corporate philanthropy:

> *Does your corporate involvement in this community benefit your company? Well, it brings benefit as a result. It is an end result. Of course, we don't participate in the activity solely for gaining benefit. Of course, as a result, for example, by participating community contribution, our employees, as I said before, we can think of it as a part of employee welfare. Or, we can think of it as helping*

to improve our brand image. Of course, our employees work under such an
~~improved brand name. It creates pride in them and motivates them. That's why,~~
as a result, I think it brings benefit.

At Kagoshima, active participation in the community has been linked to the company's business strategy as a cycle of creating a successful business. By putting an effort in corporate philanthropy, the community will be a better place in which to live; the employees who live there will improve their quality of life, and those employees who see Kagoshima's contribution to the community are proud of themselves for being a part of this company. Eventually, their motivation and morale improves, and finally, it brings efficiency in production. An example of this improvement in employees' quality of life is seen in Kagoshima's Hispanic workers. Kagoshima brought a large number of Hispanic workers with their families to Heartland when they moved their microwave oven production from Chicago. As many of them did not speak English, the Heartland/General County literacy council, which is funded by Kentucky Bluegrass United Way, operated an English program for them. A good reputation of the community as providing services for needs of the residents attracts new workers and retains skilled workers. Thus, Kagoshima can envisage that corporate philanthropy is a medium through which both the community and corporations can prosper.

AN ANALYSIS OF CORPORATE PHILOSOPHY ON GIVING

American employers B. B. Fishwater and Goodman, and Japanese company, Kagoshima, see the relationship between corporate philanthropy and the benefit to their companies, as well as to their employees. On the other hand, Japanese companies GTS and Dainichi, and British company, Fortson, do not discern the connection between corporate giving and the benefits to their companies. It seems that America has an expectation that business should be involved in community improvement activities. In response to this expectation and working to meet that expectation, the American companies started to see the benefit of doing just that. Yet, the Japanese companies and the British company have not developed an understanding of the benefit of corporate giving. The only exception is Kagoshima, which has been in the U.S. since 1959. Because of its longevity, day by day encounters, and overcoming many cultural gaps, the company has developed an understanding of the benefit in doing philanthropy.

Although the national origin of companies affects the corporate philosophy on corporate giving, the CEO's personal philosophy also affects the behavior of the company. As mentioned before, Fortson does not donate money to charity at all because it is prohibited by the headquarters in Britain. However, the president of Fortson is an American. He understands the American culture about philanthropy. He knows what is to be expected in the community. Therefore, he does not like the company policy dictated by the British parent company. He states "I am diametrically opposed to that [the British policy] because if they, the company is going to try to be in the community a long time, it's gotta give back to the community. It's just taking out from the community, it's not gonna be, it's not gonna stay long for a company." The policy of letting shareholders decide where to donate does not work in the United States. Almost all of the shareholders live in the United Kingdom, and therefore, they do not see many American communities and places where their facilities are located, and are less inclined to spend money within these American communities. The distance between the shareholders and the community attenuates the commitment of the former to the latter. Even if the shareholders live in a country where their facility is located, they are less likely to be concerned about the community in the same way managers and employees are. We have witnessed time after time their motive for short-term profit gain, which often ignored the welfare of the communities. Determining it as a company's benefit, the Fortson president plans to persuade his parent company to change its corporate giving policy by including other group companies located in the United States. He believes in corporate citizenship, and its benefits for both the community and the company. He believes it is his duty to carry out this task. He describes the benefit to the company as follows:

In the United States, our philosophy is that we have a community in which we reside, and when we reside there, we impact the environment in our community and we impact neighborhoods, not only with our physical structure, but with our employees in workforce. And our workforce, whether it lives in the area or drives through the area, we need to make sure that we are good neighbors, and by doing that, I think it makes your place a desirable place to work. So, if you need to hire people, good people want to work for you. I think if you wanted the company to be a long term survivor, you need to maintain good relationships with the other companies in the area, local governments, the media and just the general population. You know, people find out about you in two ways. One is to read bad things about you in a paper. Or, they meet your employees, and either like your employees or they don't like them. And they like you or don't like you because of what employees say about the place they work. So, as long as we are considered a good place to work because we give back to the community, I think we tend to draw better personnel, more productive personnel, and that impacts obviously our productivity of our making our product and our profitability. I think in the long run, it just makes you a stronger company.

Even though his parent company does not allow its American branch to donate money directly to charities, the president of the American branch strongly believes in corporate giving. He created a corporate culture of philanthropy, which is very active and well recognized in the community. Since the company cannot issue a check for philanthropy, he uses employee donations and in-kind donations to contribute to the community. He advocates active involvement in the community to his employees, and shows them an example of the involvement. Last year, he was the Chairman of the United Way. This year, he is the President of the Board of the United Way, and the Vice President of the Red Cross. The employees donate money and/or participate in volunteer work for the United Way, March of Dimes, Big Brothers & Big Sisters, Salvation Army, Food Trees and other organizations. Contributions of Fortson's employees are appreciated within the community. In 1999, Fortson won the Spirit Award for the Commonwealth of Kentucky from the United Way. In addition to receiving the Spirit Award, one of the employees was named the State Volunteer of the year from the United Way. These awards are the results of each employee's commitment to improve the community. In 1999, Fortson's employees donated a total of $58,100 to the United Way, which averaged out to around $200.34 per employee. This is more than Goodman employees' per capita donation of $186.97. In the same year, Goodman was the number one American donor to the United Way. It is noted that Fortson achieved its status without a corporate pledge. Fortson used, and continues to use, in-kind donations and volunteer work as a means to contribute to the community. For example, the company allows community groups to use their conference rooms when unoccupied. The company also allows many of their employees to attend charity organizations when production is slow. In 1999, the company sent 35 workers to the United Way's Day of Caring. They worked on 15 to 20 different projects ranging from helping the elderly with planting gardens, to painting the Red Cross building. In opposition to its British parent company, the American president has created an active corporate norm of philanthropy.

Non-monetary contributions by the firm are important parts of corporate social responsibility. In particular, volunteer work by the employees shows the firm's willingness to contribute to the community. In other words, it is an indication of how much they think about their community. There is a difference among corporations in how to manage volunteer work. In general, American companies are willing to support employees to be involved in volunteer work. On the other hand, Japanese companies are not as aware of the importance of volunteer work for the contribution to the community as American companies are. Table 5.1 shows comments by company managers on volunteer work. The concept of volunteerism is more positively evaluated

Table 5.1.   Comments on Volunteer Work by Firms

American Firms	Japanese Firms	A British Firm
Our people are active in civic activities through the United Way's Day of Caring, preparing for a fair. We do for Christmas time for people without family. They (United Way) ask for one day (volunteering) and what we do is we have sign-up sheet. They [employees] go out work [for the volunteering] for the day and we pay them for that day. We also have a large number of volunteers out of this plant who participate in a lot of charitable philanthropy. A lot of things outside of just work.	We don't have any system to encourage employees for volunteer work. We don't educate them for that purpose. It is a big thing to shut down factory for 30 minutes out of 8 hours for the United Way by paying that part of salary. It is a burden to our business. When the United Way asks us to release our workers for volunteer, we have to think about it thoroughly because it involves whether we should support their wages or not during they volunteer. We don't refuse the request, but we have to think about it carefully.	The day of caring we had, I think maybe only 35 people were able to participate in last year. They worked on 15 or 20 different things. I found that if I give people two hours off to go do something to help somebody or something, it does not impact at all to the amount of productivity that we have. We had almost 35 people go to the day of caring, which is 7:30AM to 1 O'clock on one day where they go out and work various projects in community.

by American companies than Japanese companies. A British company led by an American manager is very active in volunteering as a way of compensating for the lack of direct contribution by the parent company.

NORMATIVE EXPECTATIONS

Institutional theory (Scott, 1995) looks at organizational behaviors using an analytical tool of regulative, normative and cognitive structures of institutions. From a normative aspect, organizations find out what are the appropriate and expected behaviors in relation to their environment. In contrast, from a cognitive aspect, organizations construct their identities and find out what kind of actions make sense in a given situation.

In the United States, there is an expectation that corporations should be involved in community improvement activities. This normative pressure is strongly present in Heartland. For some companies, this norm, that is, active involvement of corporate philanthropic activities, is felt to be important. Therefore, they take the role of corporate citizen in this activity, and they have a good understanding of what the community expects of them. The normative pressure from the community is well taken by Heartland's corporations. They understand the relationship between corporate philanthropy and the benefit to their companies in general, as well as to recruitment & retention of employees specifically. Therefore, they construct their identity as a good corporate citizen. Goodman and B. B. Fishwater are good examples of this. These two companies participate in corporate philanthropy from both normative and cognitive structures (as shown in Table 5.2 and Figure 5.1). Both companies internalize corporate citizenship roles and identify themselves as a significant player in community improvement activities in Heartland. Kagoshima's corporate citizenship activities are also operated in normative and cognitive structures. However, because it is a Japanese corporation which needs to learn the American way of corporate social responsibility, their cognitive understanding is slightly less than Goodman and B. B. Fishwater. Kagoshima's philanthropic activities are motivated more by normative structure than Goodman and B. B. Fishwater.

The Fortson president and his employees also grasp the relationship between corporate giving and human resources management, in addition to the community expectation. They really believe in the idea and act accordingly. The president of Fortson has created a corporate identity in which employees are proud of themselves for their outstanding volunteer activities and donations.

Table 5.2. Perceptions of Corporate Giving on Retention/Recruitment

	Has Positive Effect	Has Negative Effect	No Position
B.B. Fishwater (American)	✓		
Goodman (American)	✓		
Kagoshima (Japanese)	✓		
GTS (Japanese)			✓
Dainichi (Japanese)		✓	
Fortson (British Parent)		✓	
Fortson (American President & Employees)	✓		

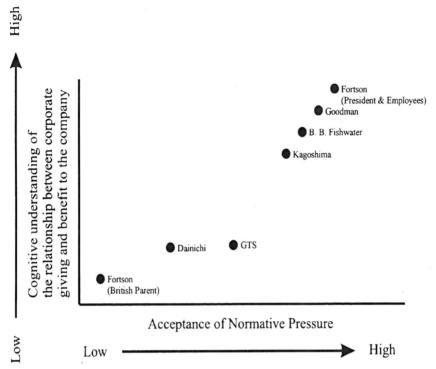

Figure 5.1. Understanding & Acceptance of Corporate Philanthropy by Selected Heartland Companies.

Dainichi, GTS and Fortson's British parent do not perceive the relationship between corporate social responsibility and retention & recruitment of workers. Therefore, it does not make sense for them to return a lot of money to the community. However, Dainichi and GTS do feel a pressure from the community, and as such, they do contribute. GTS has a more active role than Dainichi in corporate philanthropy. Because GTS has been in Heartland much longer than Dainichi, it has had more time to absorb the community's expectations. Fortson's British parent does not comprehend the norm (community expectation), nor do they understand the relationship between corporate philanthropy and the benefits to the company. Therefore, the company does not give any money to the community (as shown in Table 5.3). In sum, companies' behaviors on corporate giving in Heartland are influenced by their understanding of the relationship between corporate philanthropy and the benefits to their companies, and by their sensitivity to the community expectation.

Table 5.3. Quotes to Illustrate the Understanding and Acceptance of Corporate Philanthropy by Selected Heartland Companies

Fortson (President & Employees)	People feel good about the company they work for because it's caring, and shows that it wants to help the community. This company won the Spirit Award for the state of Kentucky last year.
Goodman	We haven't been here very long, but we have been very, very active in the community, things as far as donating time, donating money to certain, various [projects], primarily in the General County-Heartland area with actively supporting education areas, technical education growth. We've also supported most of the charities in the area.
B. B. Fishwater	We support the community where we are in. We support the people that are in those communities and we are a good community partner. We only give to the communities we are located and that's the benefit not only the community, but also to many of our employees, who are members of the community.
Kagoshima	Corporate social responsibility is a way to make business activity successful. It makes the corporation prosper. By that, employees can have better life, and the community becomes more attractive.
GTS	Corporation at least should donate a minimum amount of money. Basically, in business operation, it is not so important to do corporate philanthropy and donation. Because we have localization policy, we participate in corporate giving in America.
Dainichi	Our primary responsibility is the welfare of employees, and although community is important, it is the secondary importance. Participation to community activities does not benefit the company directly.
Fortson (Parent Company)	British parent does not allow corporate giving.

NOTES

1. An assembly plant called New United Motor Manufacturing, Inc. (NUMMI) was built in Fremont, California in 1984. This is a joint venture between General Motors and Toyota. Therefore, the first genuine Toyota plant is Toyota Motor Manufacturing Kentucky, Inc. established in 1986.

2. When Japan experienced an economic slump in the 1990s, and afterwards failed to fully recover, researchers, especially Western scholars, started to move away from studying Japanese management (Lynn, 2002), instead shifting their focus to China. Therefore, compared to the 1970s and the 1980s, there has been much less research conducted on Japanese management in recent years. However, during these years, Japanese multinational corporations are changing, as they hope to become more competitive in the world market by correcting weaknesses.

Mroczkowski and Hanaoka (1998) predict that Japanese companies are expected to adopt a universalist human resource management system, including contractual hiring and performance-based rewards. They predict that Japanese human resource management will be dissolved by the year 2010. As a part of the restructuring process, decision making is also changing, becoming less centralized and more adaptable to a changing environment (Kono and Clegg, 2001).

3. Ideally, in Japanese management, the quality of their products should be constantly improved through the commitment of their workers. The Japanese management strategies mentioned in the text are designed to encourage this commitment from workers.

Scholars such as Deming (1986) and Ebrahimpour (1988) see the difference between American and Japanese management in the area of quality control. Japanese quality management places an emphasis on employee training, in order to promote quality control ideas to other employees. This means that, in Japanese management, they associate organizational performance with quality control, with this idea permeating throughout the company. In contrast, American quality control places an emphasis on inspection. Quality control is not very important throughout the organization, only becoming so at the end of production process. In a study of Japanese corporations in the United States, Ebrahimpour and Cullen (1993) show that Japanese companies are more likely to use the promotion style of quality control than American companies. In other words, in Japanese corporations, quality control becomes a major concern for employees.

4. A resource dependence perspective suggests that organizations need to engage in exchanges with the environment in order to survive, because organizations are not capable of maintaining themselves without getting resources from the environment (Pfeffer and Salancik 1978).

5. For example, successful Japanese companies in the United States choose their production sites in depressed rural areas of southern states (Japan External Trade Organization, 1990; Yang, 1992). This is a result of the different characteristics of labor by region. Rural areas of southern states have labor forces that are less likely to unionize, and have abundant potential employees who have little work experience in American manufacturing systems. Japanese firms try to avoid people with experience in union activities. This is to say that the characteristics of a labor force in these areas are closer to the labor force that Japanese firms are seeking.

6. When considering the labor market, we also need to consider types of industry. Comparing five Japanese service firms (banks and a security firm) in New York with five Japanese manufacturing companies in Tennessee, Beechler and Yang (1994) show different degrees of adaptation to American human resource management. Japanese

service firms in New York are moving toward Americanization of the companies. In human resource management, they adopt the American human resource practices, such as hiring more specialists, more job titles, reducing internal training, instituting formal performance appraisal programs, and moving to merit-based compensation systems. They Americanize human resource management because Japanese human resource management does not function in the fluid and heterogeneous labor market of New York, and managers think that Americanizing human resource management is the only way the firms will be able to function well. American employees are not interested in job security, but higher pay and status. Also, they are professional workers who can easily find a job in another company. The labor market in Tennessee, on the other hand, is very different. The labor force is more homogeneous, and people are looking for job security and long term employment. The turnover rate in Tennessee is much lower than that of New York, and the labor force in Tennessee fits well with the requirements of the Japanese human resource management style. Since there are more job applicants to these Japanese companies in Tennessee than jobs available, they use extensive hiring procedures, including interviews, in which workers whose personalities can match well with company philosophy are hired.

Extensive hiring procedures are also observed in Japanese firms in Kentucky. For example, Toyota Motor Manufacturing Company in Kentucky is very selective in hiring. Screening takes 6 months to a year from the time of applying to actual hiring (Besser, 1998; personal interviews with Toyota employees, 2004). Toyota conducts a series of interviews to the prospective employees during that period, in order to hire the people whose personalities match well with the company's philosophy.

7. Wright describes one of the characteristics of giving in the United States as an expression of personal and social identity, and goals. This is in contrast to giving in Britain. In Britain, giving is generally peripheral to social identity and goals (Wright, 2001: 413).

8. As Japanese corporations increase the number of temporary and contract workers relative to permanent workers, their social support function has been weakened. In this situation, the government should have taken a more active role, yet they have tried to hold down the expenditure for the social security safety net in order to balance the budget. Thus, recently, there are more people who are living under poverty, are unable to receive adequate social support. In 1998, there were 7,930,000 workers whose annual income was 2 million yen. However, in 2007, that number rose to 10,320,000 (Asahi Shimbun 2009).

9. *Seken,* a basic concept that describes Japanese interpersonal relationships is a good tool to understand this kind of behavior. It is a concept that resides between *uchi* (inner group) and *soto* (outer group), and becomes a frame of reference for action. It is a basis for what Benedict (1946, 2006) identified in the Japanese culture of shame. Compared to norm and folkway, it has more weight on the inner and psychological aspect of behavioral patterns (Hamashima 2005). See Kinya Abe's "*Seken towa Nanika* (What is *Seken?*)" (1995) for more detail on *Seken.*

Chapter Six

Firm Size and Corporate Social Responsibility

THE IMPORTANCE OF FIRM SIZE IN CORPORATE GIVING

It is common sense to think that larger corporations are more active in philanthropy. We often hear the news of donations made by corporate giants such as IBM, Coca Cola, Microsoft and others. In news conferences where they announce corporate gifts, chairpersons of these large companies speak about their commitment to corporate social responsibility. Chief executive officers share an idea of the corporations' active role in society. For example, in addition to making products, the chairman of Dupont once said that "the larger it [a corporation] is, the more it is expected to assume various obligations that once were met by individuals or communities, or were not met at all"(Mitchell, 1989:2). These accounts suggest we should look at firm size as a factor in corporate giving.

Firm size has been studied as a concept to understand organizations. In organizational studies, researchers have treated firm size as a dimension of organizational structure, or an independent variable that affects the organization's structural characteristics and behaviors. It can also be seen as a dependent variable, that is, a variable which is affected by some other factors. In this research, firm size is examined as an independent variable to describe the organizational characteristics and behaviors on corporate giving. As a variable, firm size has been conceptualized in many ways. It can be sales figures, the number of branches, total square meter floor space, number of employees, amount of profit earned and so forth. Among many choices of operationalization, the number of employees is a good measure of firm size, and it is widely used in organization research. The advantage of the number of employees as a measure for firm size is that "it tends to reflect both the capacity of the organization for performing work as well as the current scale

77

of actual performance" (Scott, 1992: 259). Also, the number of employees is one of the most accessible forms of data on organizations.[1]

Corporate giving has become an essential element of business function in the United States. As described in the previous chapters, corporations practice strategic philanthropy that integrates corporate giving into their overall strategic planning of the corporation (Marx, 1998: 34). In many communities, they are expected to participate in community improvement activities in the form of corporate giving and volunteering. Various studies have looked at factors that influence the level of giving. Firm size is one such variable that many researchers have investigated as a factor. In this study, firm size as a factor for the level of giving among Japanese and American firms in an American rural community is investigated.[2]

FIRM SIZE AND FORMALIZATION

In organization theory, firm size has been used as a variable to affect organizational structure. The relationship between firm size and structural characteristics is often discussed at an abstract level; for example, research shows the relationship between firm size and the level of bureaucratization, centralization and formalization. Weberian theory of organization suggests that the larger the organization, the more formalized its structure will be. Formalization here is defined as "the extent to which roles and relationships are specified independently of the personal characteristics of the occupants of positions" (Scott, 1992:261). This prediction has been confirmed in many empirical studies. For example, Blau and Schoenheer (1971) studied state employment security agencies, and found a relationship between organizational size and the formalization as measured by the extent of written personnel regulations.

The association between company size and formalization is also mentioned in studies on corporate philanthropy. Useem (1988) contends that larger companies give more money to charitable causes than smaller companies because larger companies have more formalized contribution programs with professional staff. This relationship holds true regardless of profits. Once a formalized corporate contribution department has been established, money has to be allocated to operate the department in a budgetary process, removing the contribution money from the fluctuation of profit level. Thus, Useem found that the large companies more uniformly give near the one-to-two percent level, and they allocate funds in a more consistent way among the major groupings of non-profit organizations.

Burlingame and Frishkoff also support this relationship saying that "the likelihood that a company will have a formal contributions budget increases with the size of the company (Burlingame and Frishkoff, 1996:91)." In their studies, on average 75 percent of the large companies have a formal contribution budget, while only 20 percent of the small companies made this allocation in their budget. Brammer and Millington's study of UK firms also supports this relationship. They conclude that "the allocation of internal responsibility for the management of corporate giving is significantly influenced by the extent and type of managerially perceived stakeholder pressures, organizational size, and industry characteristics" (Brammer and Millington, 2004: 268). This means that as the size of the firm increases, charitable contributions are more likely to be managed by a delegated department, and not by the top management.[3]

As we have seen, previous research shows the association between firm size and the formalization of corporate giving. But why do large corporations make the corporate giving function formal? One reason is that, compared to smaller firms, large firms are more visible to the public, their corporate names more widely known, and their presence in communities is felt by citizens. In order to justify their commercial activities, they engage in activities of corporate social responsibility, as their business reputation affects the sales of their products. A good case to illustrate this is a study conducted in the United Kingdom in 1998. It showed that 17 percent of British adults had boycotted a company's product for ethical reasons, and 19 percent of them had chosen a product/service because of a firm's ethical reputation (Market and Opinion Research International, 2000). Corporate giving needs to be visible to the public, and forming a specific contribution department makes it easy for the public to have access to information regarding the firm.

While large firms have the resources to delegate tasks, smaller firms do not have the time or financial resources for corporate giving activities. In a study investigating South Asian businesses in the United Kingdom, Worthington and his associates (2003: 23) found that small and medium sized South Asian firms do not undertake corporate social responsibility in a formal and structured way. Rather, they engage in the activities largely in an ad hoc, informal and reactive manner. Therefore, almost all initiatives for corporate social responsibility come from the top of the organization.

This research partially supports the argument mentioned above for Japanese companies. Dainichi, the smallest Japanese company in Heartland, does not have any contribution department, either at the American plant or its headquarters in Japan. The facility in Heartland gives money to charity case by case, and there is no formal allocation of money, rather, the Vice President and Plant Manager usually handle the contribution budget. Similarly, GTS Wire and Cable, the medium sized Japanese company in Heartland, does not have any contribution department or office, either at the American plant or its headquarters in Japan. Their philanthropic activity is handled by a plant manager and some Japanese management in GTS Wire and Cable in Heartland. On the other hand, Kagoshima, the largest Japanese company in Heartland, has a contribution department in its headquarters in Japan. In addition, it established a charitable foundation in 1988, which is separate from Kagoshima itself, and its name is now well known among non-profit organizations. Kagoshima even has a corporate contribution department in its American headquarters, located in New Jersey. However, the Heartland plant does not have a department to handle corporate giving, rather, it is managed by human resources personnel and the management team. When we look at a corporation as a whole, including the parent company, the largest company has a more formalized way of undertaking philanthropic activities than medium and small sized companies.

Kagoshima, as a leading Japanese firm operating overseas, is considered a benchmark corporation for its business activities, which include corporate philanthropy, and it feels institutional pressure from the presence of other leading Japanese corporations.[4] In the 1950s, leading Japanese manufacturing firms, including Toyota, Hitachi and Kagoshima, built their sales facilities in the United States to export goods from Japan, and many of these firms have since established foundations to participate in American civil society. In this environment, a corporation tries to mimic other corporations in its organizational design and activities. This standard response to uncertainty is called mimetic isomorphism. DiMaggio and Powell say "when the environment creates symbolic uncertainty, organizations may model themselves on other organizations" (DiMaggio and Powell, 1991:69).

These leading firms faced much uncertainty when they established their facilities in the United States. In order to overcome this, they adopted some of the management styles of American firms (e.g., labor relations), while at the same time imitating other Japanese firms. To establish a foundation was a standard mimetic process of these leading Japanese firms. In contrast, GTS Wire & Cable and Dainichi, which came to the U.S. in the 1980s and the 1990s, are not leading Japanese firms, and do not feel the institutional pressure that large organizations have experienced. Thus, these small and medium sized firms have not attempted to formalize a contribution function.

FIRM SIZE AND THE LEVEL OF GIVING

Research on the relationship between firm size and the level of corporate giving has shown mixed results. Some studies (McElroy and Siegfried 1985, Tillman 1999) show a relationship that is nonlinear or has no relationship. For example, McElroy and Siegfried (1985) used data from 1970 Corporate Income Tax Returns to see the relationship between firm size and corporate giving. They used assets as a measure of firm size, and divided the companies into 14 groups of asset classes, ranging from $0 to $1 billion and over. In the asset classes sized between $0–1,000, contributions range from 0.1 to 0.6 percent of the total pre-tax net income. When the size of the asset class increases to $5 million to $50 million, the percentage of contributions also increases, by as much as 1.2 percent of pre-tax income. In the highest asset class size of $1 billion and over, contributions decrease to 0.8 percent of total pre-tax net income. These results indicate an inverted U-shaped relationship, that is, medium sized companies contributed to charitable causes the most, while small and large sized companies contributed less to charity.

Other studies (Michell 1989, Jemison 2001) indicate a positive relationship: as a company becomes larger, it makes more generous contributions. In his analysis of 1983 Fortune 500 companies, Mitchell (1989) found a clear association between the variables of size and social policy which is conceptually similar to corporate philanthropy. He used sales as a measure of company size. Among the top 100 companies, 14 had a high level of social policy commitment. On the other hand, among the 100 companies ranked between 401 and 500, only 3 companies had a high level of social policy commitment. In addition, 74 companies among the 100 firms ranked between 401 and 500 had no social policy commitment, while in contrast, only 18 of the top 100 companies had no social policy commitment. Mitchell explains this result from the institutional argument. He sees a corporation as a political institution. As a political institution, it is concerned with legitimacy as well as profit making. Corporate social responsibility is viewed as one of the important strategies needed to obtain legitimation. Because larger firms are more likely to face legitimation problems due to their visibility in society, they are more likely to be involved in activities of corporate social responsibility. In general, the institutional argument is a perspective, in which the institutional environment is seen to influence organizational structure and behavior.

Useem (1988) contends that large firms contribute more money than smaller firms, regardless of earnings, because large firms make philanthropic activity more formal and professional. We can view this formalization of corporate giving as the establishment of formal programs, a contribution department, and/or the hiring of professional staff as the firm's size grows. As described previously, this relationship between firm size and formalization was partially found in this research. The largest firm (Kagoshima) has formal corporate giving departments in its Japanese and the U.S. headquarters, while medium and small sized firms (GTS and Dainichi) do not have any formal contributions departments. It is Useem's conclusion that the relationship between size and philanthropy is derived from the pressure of the institutional environment. He says: "the driving force here is professionalization: larger firms operate more formalized programs, and their policies are more subject to the norms prevailing within the corporate community (Useem, 1988: 81)."

The firm size and legitimation problem has also been echoed in this research. The legitimation problem is a product that emerges from the interaction of an actor and the environment. In this discussion, it is the company's relationship with the community. Heartland has an expectation that large employers will act in the community accordingly. For example, the president of the Industrial Foundation emphasizes Kagoshima's large number of employees and his expectations of what they can do for the community, and this expectation is well understood by Kagoshima, being largest employer in Heartland. A Japanese human resource manager whom the author interviewed has the opinion that American society expects businesses to act philanthropically, and that the expectation is proportional to the firm's size and type of industry. The manufacturing industry faces a higher expectation to contribute to philanthropy because of their large employment from the community. Kagoshima has always been concerned with its community because its corporate decisions have a huge impact on the community. The Japanese manager describes his perspective on the relationship between firm size, community and corporate contribution as follows:

> Well, we can't deny that what our company does will directly affect the community of Heartland. That's why, when we decide policies of corporate activities, which include a big change in policies, we need to keep in mind the community. This is what top management in this company thinks about. For example, when the business is down and we need to decrease the number of employees, we have to think about the community as a primary concern. When the company becomes very huge like this company, unconsciously, it will create a large impact on society. In response to this concern, we have to work on corporate contribution accordingly.

All managers in Japanese companies interviewed for this study mention size as a critical factor for their philanthropic behaviors. To put it succinctly, they believe that size is associated with the level of corporate giving: the bigger the organization, the greater the corporate contribution. A manager at Dainichi mentioned many times that the size of the company has been a main reason for its corporate giving behaviors. Dainichi is a small company compared to GTS Wire & Cable and Kagoshima. Not only is the employment in Heartland small, but so too is Dainichi's employment worldwide, totaling just 644 people in its four manufacturing facilities located in Shiga, Saitama and Fukui prefectures in Japan, and in Heartland. In total, Dainichi has 47 branches and sales offices, including one sales office in Indonesia. The manager is apologetic about his company's small contribution, yet, he rationalizes that it is no problem to be a small contributor for this size of the company because the company is doing the best they can, given its size. He says that:

> *Does our company fully respond to the society's expectation on corporate philanthropy? Yes, we fully respond to it. Well, I think, as a company, we do contribute to the society as much as we can for the size.*

> *Are we different from other Japanese companies in Heartland on corporate social responsibility? Yes, we are different from them and the primary reason for that is our firm size.*

Because all the companies interviewed for this study were reluctant to reveal their actual figures on corporate giving, only estimates can be made to assess their level of contribution. One of the sources is the United Way's campaign statistics. Each year, the United Way holds a campaign to raise money in each community, and this provides a good source of information on which to estimate the levels of contribution. However, it must be remembered that donations to the United Way are only one part of a corporation's giving. There are other large non-profit organizations, such as Big Brothers and Big Sisters, Walk America March of Dimes, and American Cancer Society, which also receive contributions, which they usually seek directly from the business. In addition, there are also various local non-profit organizations that seek corporate giving. In Heartland, the Kentucky School for the Deaf and the Erickson McIntosh Regional Medical Center are examples. Also, local police and fire departments and the Chamber of Commerce usually ask for donations in many communities. Therefore, it can be assumed that the Japanese corporations have many recipients to which they have donated, so care must be taken when interpreting data from the United Way campaign statistics alone. Nevertheless, in this case, a level of corporate giving by these corporations can still be inferred, because, as described in the previous chapter, the United Way has a significant presence in Heartland. Community and business leaders in Heartland refer to the United Way when they talk about corporate giving, and they are proud of having such a strong United Way organization in the community. Moreover, many business leaders in Heartland stated that the majority of their budgets in corporate giving go to the United Way. Because Japanese corporations tend to follow the norm of the society, they also affirm the importance of the United Way in the community. Kagoshima's corporate contribution department in its U. S. headquarters has a policy that shows a preferred treatment of the United Way. For example, the policy states that "United Way is the only [organization] approved [for] employee solicitation (consideration will be given to other organizations on a case-by-case basis)."

The United Way's 1999 fundraising campaign shows that Kagoshima donated $81,802 in total to the United Way (as shown in Table 6.1). Of this amount, the company's share was $25,845 (31.59 %), and the employees' share was $55,957 (68.41 %). GTS Wire and Cable donated a total of $26,087 to the United Way. The corporate pledge was $6,000 (23.00 %), while the employees pledged $22,087 (67.00 %). Dainichi donated $1,996 in total to the United Way. The company's share was $1,400 (70.13 %) and the employees donated $596 (29.87 %).

In terms of donations per employee, Kagoshima's donations were the highest, at $51.13 per person. GTS Wire & Cable and Dainichi donated almost the same amount of money per employee, with the former employees contributing $39.29 per person, and the latter $39.15. These numbers show that Kagoshima, the biggest Japanese company in Heartland, made the largest contribution in both the total amount and per employee. Because GTS Wire & Cable is larger than Dainichi, GTS Wire & Cable's total donations to the United Way were greater than Dainichi's. However, per employee, GTS Wire & Cable donated only 14 cents more than Dainichi. Although it is hard to see the impact of firm size on corporate giving when comparing medium and small sized companies, a difference in corporate philanthropy is revealed: the largest company contributes more to the

Table 6.1.   1999 Kentucky Bluegrass United Way Fundraising Campaign Statistics, Japanese Manufacturing Companies

Company	Total Contribution (USD)	Corporate Pledge (USD)	Employee Pledge (USD)	Number of Employees	Contribution Per Employees (USD)
Kagoshima	$81,802.54	$25,845	$55,957.54	1,600	$51.13
GTS Wire & Cable	$26,087.03	$6,000	$22,087.96	664	$39.29
Dainichi	$1,996.4	$1,400	$596.4	51	$39.15

(Kentucky Bluegrass United Way, 2000)

charity than medium and small sized companies. This finding is in accordance with Lombardo's research, in which she asserted that Japanese philanthropic activities in the United States show an association between firm size and corporate contribution. She says that "the degree of participation by Japanese companies in corporate contribution in the United States is strongly correlated with their size and the length of time they have been operating here (Lombardo, 1991:16)."

Except for the largest corporations, many Japanese companies are relatively inactive in corporate giving. Large corporations, such as Toyota and Hitachi, have been in business in the United States since late 1950s, and are not only the largest Japanese employers, but also the pioneers in doing business in the United States. They are the ones who are active in corporate philanthropy in the Unites States, and have successfully transplanted their businesses to the United States (as shown in Table 6.2). Except for Lombardo's findings, we do not have any other data on the philanthropic activities of medium and small sized Japanese companies. Lombardo's suggestion that Japanese corporations, except large ones, are inactive is implied by a survey conducted by Bob and his associates (1991). In a question that asks: "Which of the following, if any, are barriers to your affiliate's greater participation in corporate citizen activities?" the category Japanese companies answered the most was "We do not have the manpower to manage corporate citizenship activities." It was followed by "My affiliate does not have the financial resources for these activities." These two answers are closely related with firm size. Based on the findings from this and others'

Table 6.2. Age, Size and Contributions of Major Japanese Corporations in the United States

Company	Established in United States	Number of U.S. Employees, 1988–89	1989 Contributions (millions of USD)
Union Bank	1952	7,300	$ 1.2
Toyota	1957	5,500	$ 1.4
Kagoshima	1959	9,000	$ 1.1
Hitachi	1959	6,000	$ 1.7
American Honda	1959	7,300	$ 0.6
Subaru	1968	1,100	$ 0.4

Note: With the exception of Kagoshima, estimates include both contributions made by the foundation, if the corporation has one, and directly by the corporation. They do not include contributions made in the United States by parent companies in Japan, nor do they include certain large, one-time grants. Kagoshima's figure is foundation only. Kagoshima committed to donating 0.1 % of U.S. sales to U.S. not-for-profits. This could amount to over $4 million annually in direct company contributions, in addition to those made by the foundation.
(This table is adopted from Lombardo, 1991)

research, it is fair to say that, for Japanese companies, significantly large
organizations are more likely to donate to charitable causes than medium
and small sized companies.

It is important here to touch upon the issue of firm size as a causal factor.
The question of whether or not firm size is irrelevant, and whether higher
wage earners contribute more than those with lower wages, is a challenge
to the relationship between firm size and the level of contribution. There
are two ways to address this question. First, if one can demonstrate that
wage level does not have a relationship with the contribution level, this
question becomes less relevant. Unfortunately, only the wage level from
Kagoshima was made available to this study, but not that of Dainichi and
GTS Wire & Cable. Therefore, we cannot know the relationship between
the wage level and the level of contribution. However, if one could get data
on wage levels, there are two possible conclusions. The first possibility
is that there is no relationship between wage level and contribution. The
second possibility is that there is a relationship between wage level and
contribution. In this case, the question may appear to be reasonable. However, a second approach to the question can make it irrelevant if we can
establish causation. That is, if we can demonstrate that firm size is a cause
of wage level, we can refute the irrelevancy of size claim in the question.
Regardless of whether size directly influences contributions, or size influences contribution through wage, size does matter. So, if we can establish
the relationship between firm size and wage level, the question becomes
invalid. In labor studies, it is a well known empirical fact that large firms
pay higher wages than smaller ones in the United States (Miller and Mulvey, 1996; Brown and Medoff, 1989). The larger the firm, the higher the
wages (as shown in Table 6.3). Therefore, although the question, "could
it be possible that firm size may be irrelevant, wouldn't higher wage job
earners contribute more than lower wage earners?" looks reasonable, the
empirical fact shows that the question is invalid.

Table 6.3.   Firm Size and Payroll Per Employee in the United States, 1998

Firm Size (Number of Employees)	Number of Employees Nationwide (in thousand)	Annual Payroll (billion USD)	Income Per Employee
20 or less	25,785	608	$23,579.6
20 to 99	29,202	696	$23,834
100 to 499	25,364	675	$26,612.5
500 to 999	7,021	219	$31,192.1
1000 or more	12,962	467	$36,028.4

(This table is created based on data from the Statistical Abstract of the United States, 1998)

FIRM SIZE AND CORPORATE GIVING IN THE CASE
OF AMERICAN FIRMS IN KENTUCKY

Now, going back to the main discussion, compared to Japanese companies, when we look at American corporations, the association between corporate size and the level of corporate giving is not as clear. Table 6.4 shows all the American manufacturing companies located in Heartland, listed in the order of ranking in number of employees. In the last column, a ranking by the amount of contribution per employee is shown. When we compare these two rankings, it indicates that, in general, there is no relationship between firm size and the level of corporate giving to the United Way. For example, B. B. Fishwater, the largest American employer in Heartland, ranks sixth in terms of contribution per employee, donating $104.32. Meanwhile, Huntsman, which is the fourth largest American employer in Heartland's manufacturing industry, ranks eighth in the amount of corporate giving per employee, donating $91.45 per employee. On the other hand, Dancing Corporation, which employs 112 people and ranks seventh in the number of employees, donated $164.42 per employee, ranking second in the corporate giving category. Goodman, which ranks tenth in the number of employees, donated the most to the United Way, with $186.97 per employee. However, this is not surprising because of Goodman's unique position in the community, being a subsidiary of a giant corporation. Although it employs only 100 people in Heartland, the parent company, Goodman Incorporated, has a total employment of 66,000 worldwide, with 34,338 inside the U.S. as of 1999. Thus, the number one status in the amount of contribution per employee is not unusual. No association between firm size and corporate giving was further supported by this study's interviews.[5] In contrast to Japanese corporations, which mentioned size as a contributing factor for philanthropy, no American corporation mentioned size as an important factor for their behavior in corporate giving.

Although the scale of company size is different, a survey of corporate contributions in 1997, conducted by the Conference Board (1999), supports the findings of this study, revealing that there is no relationship between firm size and corporate giving (as shown in Table 6.5). Companies with less than 1,000 employees, the smallest category in the survey, contributed $426 per employee. This is more than the medium sized or largest categories. In the medium sized categories, for example, companies with employment between 2,500 and 4,999 contributed $280 per employee. Companies with more than 50,000 employees donated $339 per employee.

Here, it is necessary to comment on the scale used for the company size. In this research, small sized companies are less than 100 employees, while

Table 6.4. 1999 Kentucky Bluegrass United Way Fundraising Campaign Statistics, American Manufacturing Companies

Company	Number of Employees	Rank In Number of Emp.	Total Contribution (USD)	Contribution Per Employee (USD)	Rank In the Amount of Contribution Per Employee
B. B. Fishwater	1,010	1	$105,358.24	$104.32	6
Blue Wing Shoe Co.	280	2	$45,012.73	$160.76	5
DANA	200	3	$32,272.96	$161.36	3
Huntsman	175	4	$16,003	$91.45	8
Jackson Furniture	150	5	$24,160.26	$161.07	4
AdMart	135	6	$12,788.61	$94.73	7
Dancing Co.	112	7	$18,414.63	$164.42	2
Penn Ventilator	100	8	$1,272.52	$12.73	11
Burkmann Mills	95	9	$4,143.72	$43.62	9
Goodman	90	10	$16,826.92	$186.97	1
Sellers Engineering	80	11	$1,501	$18.76	10
Fred Cain Farm Equip.	36	12	NA	NA	—
DAVCO	15	13	NA	NA	—

Note: There is no data on the contributions made by Fred Cain Farm Equipment and DAVCO. This could possibly be due to the fact that their contributions were too small, or they did not contribute to the United Way at all. (Based on data from Kentucky Bluegrass United Way, 2000)

Table 6.5.   U.S. Contributions per Employee, 1997, by Employee Size Group, Medians

Number of Employees	Amount of Contribution (USD)
Less than 1,000	$426
1,000–2,499	$496
2,500–4,999	$280
5,000–9,999	$389
10,000–14,999	$303
15,000–24,999	$542
25,000–49,999	$438
50,000 or more	$339
Total All Companies	$369

(The Conference Board, 1999)

large sized companies are between 1,000 and 2,000 employees. In the study conducted by the Conference Board, small companies were less than 1,000 employees, while the largest companies consist of 50,000 or more employees. In terms of the organization vs. the environmental relationships, the sample organizations in the Conference Board study are representatives of corporations in the United States. In this study, the sample organizations are representatives of corporations in the city of Heartland. Therefore, the relationships are companies vs. society for the Conference Board study, and companies vs. community for this study. Regardless of the difference in the environment (i.e.: society vs. community), it should be noted that the environment presents norms affecting organizational behaviors. In this case, both society and community have an influence on the corporate giving.

INSTITUTIONALIZATION OF CORPORATE GIVING

I have suggested that American manufacturing companies in Heartland did not indicate a relationship between firm size and corporate giving. On the other hand, Japanese manufacturing companies in Heartland indicated a partial relationship between firm size and corporate giving. Why is this so? One way to understand this phenomenon is through a discussion of institutions. Here, institutions mean social orders or patterns that "when chronically reproduced, owe their survival to relatively self-activating social processes" (Jepperson, 1991:145).

As discussed in this study's literature review (chapter 2), corporate social responsibility has been gradually institutionalized in American society. Now, in Heartland, American corporations act as such. Just as corporations must obey laws and regulations in order to maintain their corporate life, which is essential regardless of the size, the same is also true for the corporate giving culture in Heartland. American firms are active in corporate philanthropy because that is how things are done in Heartland. Corporations do not ask why they have to donate money to community activities: when campaign season begins, companies automatically pledge donations and participate in volunteer works. Being a social fixture each year, corporate philanthropy has thus been institutionalized well in American companies, and as such, size disappears as a factor in influencing their corporate giving behavior.

In the case of Japanese companies, corporate giving is not as well institutionalized. Table 6.6 shows the comparison of institutionalization among research subjects operationalized as organizational structures. Although Japanese understand corporate philanthropy theoretically, they have not really grasped its importance. In other words, their degree of institutionalization on corporate social responsibility is lower than that of their American counterparts.

When we identify corporate giving as peripheral activities, that is, activities that are not directly related to production processes (as is the main thinking of Japanese corporations), the larger the corporation, the more it tends to consider its contribution, because the larger corporations have more room (money and human resources) for peripheral activities. As mentioned previously, two major barriers to Japanese company's greater participation in corporate citizenship activities are a lack of manpower and financial resources, which are both associated with firm size. Since corporate giving is not as well institutionalized within Japanese corporations, corporate giving, as a peripheral activity, is avoided. In an environment where corporate giving is not well institutionalized, carrying out such activities will be influenced by firm size.

Institutionalization of corporate giving by American companies has the result of a process of accepting the concept's ideal, since American organizations have not always seen corporate giving as necessary. In earlier years

Table 6.6.   Institutionalization of Corporate Giving in terms of Organizational Structures

	A Specific Department	Designated Individuals	No Set Structure
B. B. Fishwater (American)	✓	✓	
Goodman (American)	✓	✓	
Kagoshima (Japanese)	✓	✓	
GTS (Japanese)		✓	✓
Dainichi (Japanese)		✓	✓
Fortson (British)		✓	✓

of corporate America, corporate philanthropy was criticized as depriving a corporation of its resources (a representative of this argument is by Friedman, 1971). In essence, there has been a gradual acceptance of philanthropy in corporate America. Strategic management of corporate philanthropic activities can be a rational explanation for the importance of the institutionalization of corporate social responsibility. This is to integrate corporate philanthropy into an overall corporate strategy which strives to increase profitability.

Davis' (1971) two arguments against Corporate Social Responsibility (CSR) are not as persuasive anymore. The first argument relates to a lack of social skills. Opponents to CSR argued that managers cannot do well in solving social problems since they are not trained in those skills. Now, corporations entrust these jobs to federated agencies such as the United Way. Such connections to these federated agencies enable the loan executives and employees to contribute to non-profit organizations as volunteers. By doing so, employees as well as executives gain skills in dealing with social affairs. Also, many corporations have established CSR departments and hired professionals. Therefore, this argument against CSR is no longer convincing. The second argument against CSR was the cost of social involvement. Because resources were channeled to things other than economic competitiveness, it was believed to be of no benefit to the company. However, according to Fortson's president, donating money to private agencies is cheaper than paying taxes to the government and letting them take care of social affairs. This idea is widely shared by leaders in the private sector. It should also be noted that creating a good corporate identity increases competitiveness within the market.

Among American corporations, there are some differences in how corporate giving is perceived depending on the industry. Nelson (1970) indicates that labor intensive firms are more likely to participate in corporate giving than capital intensive firms, because labor intensive companies feel more responsibility to the communities in which their employees live (cited by Wolch, 1995). When corporations care about their employees, they are also more likely to care about their communities. This kind of feeling was observed in Heartland. For example, in the retail sector, especially chain stores, is not a big contributor in Heartland, and community leaders mentioned a feeling of discontent regarding the retail chain stores that do not contribute to the community. Retail stores hire transient workers and do not need to invest a lot in employees, and it is not important whether employees are skilled or not because skill levels do not affect their sales. On the other hand, in manufacturing, to obtain and retain skilled workers is a critical part of the production processes, and as such, spending time and money for employees is important. Manufacturing companies are concerned with employee satisfaction, since it lowers turnover rates. American managers in the manufacturing industry have found a relationship between community improvement activities and employee satisfaction. In a broader perspective, this relationship can be seen as a component of a corporation's enlightened self-interest. They see the benefits in participating in corporate philanthropy.

Looking at Table 6.1 and Table 6.4, with some exceptions, we see American companies donate considerably more money to the United Way than Japanese companies, in terms of the amount per employee. When combined, the three Japanese companies have a total employment figure of 2,315, and in total they donated $109,885.97 to the United Way. This means that each employee donated $47.42 to the United Way. Comparatively, the total employment of all American companies (excluding NA companies) was 2,427, with donations totaling $277,754.59 to the United Way, or $114.44 per employee. This means that American companies contributed to the United Way 2.4 times more than Japanese firms. These findings also support the argument that corporate social responsibility has been well institutionalized among American manufacturing companies when compared to their Japanese counterparts, which have less institutionalization of corporate philanthropy.

NOTES

1. The weakness of the measure is found when it measures labor intensive organization versus capital intensive organization. For example, when we look at the impact of firm size based on this measure for banks and shoe makers, it can create problems. Although banks may have fewer employees than shoes makers, the scale of performance in terms of profit and other indicators will be bigger in banks. In this research, only manufacturing companies are dealt with. It means that we deal with a similar level of labor intensiveness, therefore, the number of employees as a measure of firm size will not diminish the validity of this research.

2. Here, for the level of corporate giving, we use the amount of monetary donation to charity for its operationalization.

3. Large organizations also suffer their efficient delivery of services when they adopt central management. (Here, services mean corporate giving.) When they use decentralized management that encourages specialization of labor, the delivery of services improves (Brammer and Millington, 2004: 274).

4. Institutional theory stresses the importance of institutional pressure from a firm's external environment for the blueprint of organizational structures and responses (Meyer and Rowan, 1977).

5. This finding is in line with a study by Logan (1994), which showed no association between firm size and corporate giving.

Chapter Seven

Civil Society in Japan and the United States

INTRODUCTION

Recently, there has been a growing interest in civil society in Japan, the United States and other nations. In Japan, this has manifested in a social trend toward smaller government, with the slogan "public affairs that the private should bear," and asks for more utilization of civil society by the government. This is mainly due to the Japanese government's dire need to balance the nation's budget.

Not only is civil society emphasized by the government, but so too is its importance stressed by citizens in such fields as community development, carried out by NGOs (non-governmental organizations) and NPOs (non-profit organizations). In this section, civil society, which is an important sphere for understanding corporate philanthropy, will be described, with special focus on the difference in the constitution of civil society between Japan and the United States.

INCREASING INTEREST IN CIVIL SOCIETY

There are many associations that help local people in American communities. The activities of those associations vary, ranging from care for the elderly, job training, and youth development to care for the homeless. These organizations are called "non-profit organizations," "the independent sector," "civil society," or "voluntary organizations." Recently, the word "civil society" has attracted many scholars and policy makers as a key concept to increase the quality of life of people in the age of globalization.

The first sign of interest in civil society was in Communist countries in Eastern Europe, where the idea of civil society was used as a basis for anti-communism and the social movements for democracy. It was thought that civil society would be the springboard for the emancipation from totalitarianism in the movements for democracy. As the concept opposed to totalitarianism, the idea of civil society included "limited government," theoretically and practically (Rosenblum 2002). The use of the private sector for public affairs comes from the positive side of this idea of "limited government."

The next sign of interest in civil society was related to concerns over the growing social and economic contradictions that have gushed out from the process of globalization. Neoliberalism, often called "neo-liberal consensus," which has guided the economic policies of the world over the past 30 years, has widened the gap between the 'haves' and the 'have-nots' and wrought much environmental destruction (Salamon, 1999). The acceleration of globalization, along with neoliberalism, reveals signs of a polarization that shrinks the middle class in many countries, also bringing with it spatial patterns of uneven development. Citizens confronted with the impact of the negative aspects of globalization have found hope in the grass-roots nature of civil society for ameliorating the deteriorating aspects of their life. There are growing civil society activities in advanced societies, such as community-based environmental protection and slow-food movements for safer and environmentally friendly foods, and in developing societies, such as NGO projects in development, health and welfare.

When we look at Japan, we also see a growing interest in civil society. However, it differs from the West in terms of time and formation. Interest in voluntary activities has grown since the 1990s, spawned on by a concern for the aging population, recession and the declining rate of arrests. Together, these contributed to a declining trust in the central government, which reached a peak when the Great Hanshin earthquake in 1995 killed 6,434 people, injured 43,792 people and brought more than 300,000 refugees. The government was incapable of ameliorating the plight of affected people in the earthquake, so it was the people who brought food, money and a helping hand to those who needed it. This ignited voluntarism in Japan, and a substantial growth in volunteer activities followed. As such, the year 1995 is considered as the first year of Japanese volunteering (Economic Planning Agency, The Government of Japan, 2000).

Through these social events and trends, the social expectations of civil society reached a stage where legislation was needed. In December 1998, Law to Promote Specific Nonprofit Activities (the NPO Law) was enacted, which allowed non-profit organizations (NPOs) to be registered as public corporations. This was followed by the Nursing Care Insurance Program in April 2004, which was a response to the growing number of aged people. The program attempts to support the aged through society as a whole, and allows NPOs to participate in nursing care activities.

The number of NPOs has since grown rapidly (as shown in Chart 7.1). As of December 2005, there were 24,763 NPOs[1] (Research Institute of Economy, Trade and Industry 2005), and by February 2005, 56 percent of the NPOs were engaged in welfare (mostly nursing care) activities (Asahi Shimbun, February 16, 2005).

Although social expectation of civil society peaked during the Great Hanshin earthquake, it had in fact been gradually fermenting between the late 1980s and the early 1990s. Hasegawa et al. (2007) describe the processes of how social expectation for civil society in Japan developed, arguing that citizen activists, scholars and business elites instituted social expectation for civil society through the practice of public conversation and joint action in the early 1990s, and was supplemented by a wide coverage of the phenomena in media. In 1993, a group led by Noriyoshi Yamaoka, who later established Japan NPO Center, started research on the development of infrastructure for citizens' public interest activities at the National Institute for Research Advancement (NIRA), a policy oriented quasi-government institution. The social expectation of civil society was concretely expressed to the government in the form of a legal proposal (1994) and a research report (1996) by NIRA (Hasegawa et al.: 192). Also, Masaaki Honma (Professor of Osaka University), who later founded Japan NPO Research Association, initiated the NPO Research Forum in 1993. In 1994, Akira Matsubara and his associates established Seeds, a group that devises systems that support civic action. These three groups united to pressure the government for the NPO Law (Asahi Shimbun, February 9, 2008).

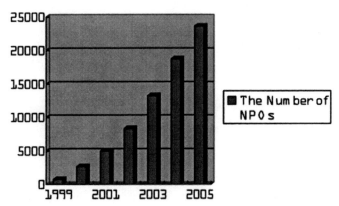

Chart 7.1. The Number of Non-Profit Organizations (NPOs) in Japan. Note: This is created from the data obtained from Research Institute of Economy, Trade and Industry. Each year, September was used to count the number. The exception is the year 2005, when December count was used.

As Hasegawa et al pointed out; the social expectation for civil society was not initiated by the government. However, the move was beneficial for the government as it tried to lessen its financial burden on welfare. Thus, the government actively participated in the discussion on preferential tax treatment for non-profit organizations. As described, the establishment of infrastructure for the activities of nonprofit organizations in Japan is very recent. This is in contrast to the tax preference for NPOs in the United States, which was instituted as the Tax Code, Section 501(c) (3) long before Japan began its discussions on the matter.

WHAT IS CIVIL SOCIETY?

What is this civil society that has attracted so many people? In this section, we will review this concept. First of all, it is understood that it is a concept opposed to the concept of government, as it includes the word "civil." Actually, for some researchers, society is composed of the two areas of government and civil society, and this distinction is made by two characteristics: the public and the private (as shown in the first figure in Figure 7.1). In this case, because enterprises are private organizations, they are regarded as a part of civil society. However, researchers' discussions have been divided as to whether the business sector should be included in civil society or not (Rosenblum 2002). In another idea, researchers look at civil society as "the third sector": a separate component of society from the government and business sectors (as shown in the second figure in Figure 7.1). For those researchers who expect civil society's power to restrain or correct the social injustices brought about by the neo-liberal consensus, it is a dominant idea to exclude the business sector from the definition of civil society. In other words, civil society is regarded as a realm in which the excesses caused by multinational corporations, which are a major component of the neo-liberal consensus, are mitigated.

This paper adopts the concept of society that separates the business sector from civil society, because many enterprises are not directly participating in social contribution activities, but are participating in the activities through nonprofit organizations. This makes the characteristics of nonprofit organizations different from those of business organizations. Therefore, society has three sectors, the government, the business sector and civil society. Concrete contributors to civil society are groups such as NPOs. There is no clear boundary between these three sectors, as NPOs' activities are often financed by the government and/or corporations (as shown in the second figure in Figure 7.1, which indicates the overlapping areas of each sector). For example, the government entrusts NPOs with nursing care services. Also, the business

1. A View of Society, Composed of Two Sectors

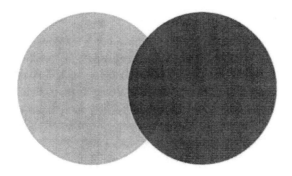

Key:

 Civil Society (including the business sector)

 The Government

2. A View of Society, Composed of Three Sectors

Key:

 The Business Sector

 Civil Society

 The Government

Figure 7.1.   A Conceptual Sketch of Civil Society.

sector provides social services to people through NPOs, so philanthropy is a good mechanism to carry out this task.

Salamon identifies five common features in civil society: organizations, private, not-for-profit distributing, self-governing, and voluntary (Salamon 1999). Civil society has organizations, and as such it exists both institutionally and structurally. The second feature, private, indicates that entities in civil society are institutionally separated from the state. Unlike business organizations, the very quality of not-for-profit distributing asks them not to yield profits to their managers or owners. The self-governing characteristic of civil society expresses that they are in charge of their own matters. The final feature, voluntary, means that membership is not legally demanded, and people are attracted to spend time and money voluntarily for causes. Surveying the discussion of civil society, Rosenblum (2002) concludes that an ideal type of civil society is a voluntary association in which a member's status in an organization is based on mutual agreement, and any member can secede at any time. As mentioned above, this study adopts an operational definition that considers civil society as voluntary associations that are separated from the government and the market.

DIFFERENCES OF THE IDEA ON CIVIL SOCIETY BETWEEN JAPAN AND THE UNITED STATES

Figure 7.2 is a conceptual sketch of the role of each sector concerning social contribution. The difference of the circles in terms of the size and the intersection varies depending on the country. For instance, the size of civil society in the United States is larger than that of Japan. In 1995, 7.8 percent of employees in the United States worked in nonprofit organizations; in contrast, only 3.5 percent of employees belonged to nonprofit organizations in Japan (Salamon 1999). Moreover, there is a close relationship between civil society and business in the United States, which is in contrast to a weak relationship between the two in Japan. (In Figure 7.2, this is indicated by the size of the black dotted area that represents corporate philanthropy.) This contrast is due to the difference in each society's approach to corporate philanthropy. In the United States, corporations contributed 450 billion dollars a year to nonprofit organizations in the latter half of the 1980s. On the other hand, corporations in Japan donated only 55 million dollars to nonprofit organizations in 1986 (Lombardo 1991). With regard to the relationship between the government and civil society, Japan and the United States show a similar pattern, that is, various subsidies flow from the government to nonprofit organizations. In the case of Japan, the government entrusted the tasks, and welfare in particular,

1. American Society

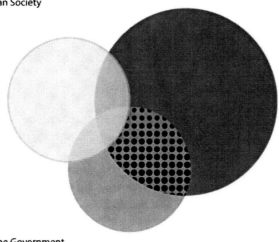

Key:

⬜	The Government
⬜	The Business Sector
⬛	Civil Society
⬛	Corporate Philanthropy

2. Japanese Society

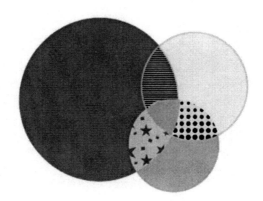

Key:

⬜	Civil Society
⬜	The Business Sector
⬛	The Government
⬛	Corporate Philanthropy
⬛	Joint ventures between government & private corporations
⬛	NPO & public interest corporation activities, such as welfare, subsidized by the gov.

Figure 7.2.   A Conceptual Sketch of the Role of Each Sector in Social Contribution.

to public interest corporations. Since the enforcement of the NPO Law in December 1998, an increasing number of NPOs have also taken on the responsibility. (The second figure in Figure 7.2 represents Japanese society. The line shaded area indicates the activities of public interest corporations and NPOs which are subsidized by the government.[2])

It is important to examine why the above mentioned difference between the countries exists. Essentially, the Japanese view of civil society differs from that of Americans, as the former has a greater expectation that government and family will play an important role in improving the quality of life than the latter. This ideal is rooted in the history and the culture of Japan, which has been influenced by the Confucianism that guided both the government and the family's role in social welfare. In the Edo period (1603–1867), it was the samurai class that received the influence of Confucianism. As elites in the Meiji era came from the former samurai class, the influence of Confucianism was maintained, even in the development period of the modern state. In this culture, it was thought that laws and institutions should be given from above (Nosco 2002). Confucianism instructs that rulers should be involved in charitable causes, in exchange for loyalty they receive from people (Hendry 1995). Therefore, the government was expected to provide people with at least the minimum standard of living, with ruler and/or the government being regarded as the parents of people and society in a pseudo-family system.

Confucianism also influenced the family. Historically, Japan established a unique institution called *ie,* which in simple terms translates to 'household' in English, but in Japanese indicates a quasi-kinship unit, in which a patriarchal head has family members connected by blood, adoption and in-law relationships. The head of household was responsible for taking care of his family members, in exchange for his absolute power within the family. Although, the institution was abolished by GHQ after World War II, the idea still persists in many group identities (Nakane, 1970: 7). It is unlikely that this aspect of Confucian culture has completely disappeared in contemporary Japan, and thus it is natural to think that it still provides an ethical base for the country (Reischauer and Jansen 1995).

The Japanese government has practiced social welfare through social welfare corporations that belong to public interest corporations or NPOs. Although social welfare corporations are non-profit organizations, in reality, they should be regarded as quasi-governmental organizations, to which services are consigned by the central and local governments (Amenomori and Yamamoto 1998). This means that Japanese voluntary associations are not genuine when contrasted to Rosenblum's ideal type of civil society. These organizations depend on the government, and in fact, 80–90 percent of their total revenue comes from the government. Although there is willingness to

move towards a smaller government, the government basically views that it
is their responsibility to engage in social welfare, and the people also expect
protection from the government.[3]

On the role of family in social welfare, Confucianism, together with
Buddhism, took a significant role in shaping the ideas. Confucianism and
Buddhism preach the importance of "repaying an obligation" to parents and
teachers. Thus, historically, aged people have been taken care of by family
members, and this tradition still survives today. For example, analyzing data
from the International Social Survey Programme (ISSP) of 2001, Akiyoshi
(2006) found that support networks among Japanese are more family-and
kinship-based than those among Americans, and Japanese are more likely to
live with their parents, children and siblings than Americans. Recent interests
in civil society, which have manifested in the enforcement of the NPO Law
and the growth of nonprofit organizations, indicate a declining importance
of the role of family in social welfare, as Japan experiences an increase in
single family households and an aging population. In terms of Figure 7.2,
the conceptual sketch, this means that the realm of civil society is gradually
expanding.

With regard to the relationship between business and civil society, Japanese
people do not expect much contribution to social welfare from the business
sector. When asked what they view philanthropy to be, many Japanese tend to
think of monetary contributions to cultural events and education. It appeared
as *mecenat* activities (patronage of literature and the arts, a French word that
Japanese use for a certain area of philanthropic activities) by large corporations before Japan went under the recession in the 1990s. Until recently, the
importance of making contributions to the homeless, the handicapped or the
poor has failed to be recognized by the Japanese, as it was considered that the
safety net of social welfare is traditionally the responsibility of the government and family (London 1991).[4] Like the government and family, Japanese
corporations have also been influenced by Confucian ideology, and have
been the major providers of safety nets to their employees, providing housing
allowances, contributions to medical insurance premiums, pensions, and so
forth. Here, like family, the safety net is limited to the members of the group.
For the general population, social welfare has been expected to be carried out
by the government. Corporations have not been concerned about the social
welfare of general population.

Recently, the role of corporations as safety net providers to their employees
is falling apart, as they shift their employment system to a more flexible one.
Faced with the recession after the collapse of bubble economy, *Keidanren*
(Japan Federation of Economic Organizations), a powerful leading business
organization in Japan, issued a guideline called "The Japanese Management

in a New Era: A Portfolio of Employment." In this guideline, *Keidanren* insisted that the Japanese employment system, represented by life-time employment and promotion based on seniority, be abolished. It called for a flexible employment system, consisting of three types of employment. The first type is the employment of a very small group of people who are entitled to carry out long-term knowledge accumulation. This type of employment is limited to those who are executive candidates in the future. The second type is the employment of a group of people who have advanced specialist knowledge, but are not necessarily guaranteed long-term employment. The third type is employment in which workers are hired flexibly based on fixed contracts and type of duties. This guideline altered the Japanese employment system greatly, bringing with it much inequality in society (Rural Culture Association 2007). Although largely a response to the recession and increasing international competition, it was also an effusion of self-interest, and a sharp move away from Confucian ideology by corporations. They reduced regular employees by 32 %, at the same time increasing part-time and contract workers by 35 %, in order to elude the burden of insurance premium and other costs (NHK 2008). Thus, the safety net supported by corporations has shrunk, which in turn has generated the problem of inadequate social security for many people. In Japan, corporations partially surrendered their social responsibility by cutting their employees, and at the same time, they have reduced their engagement in social welfare activities.[5] Thus, corporate philanthropy in Japan, small as it is when compared to the United States, has been declining even further.

In contrast, the United States has built a strong tradition of voluntary association. Tocqueville, a French political thinker and historian who traveled around the United States in 1833, observed a tendency to build voluntary associations of many different types in the country. This tradition still continues, and the United States has the most comprehensive range and largest number of nonprofit organizations in the world (Hustedde 1997). Historically, many nation-building projects were carried out by individuals, not by the government (Eberly 2000). Americans saw the strong central government with suspicious eyes, and they emphasized home rule and private initiative. The elites, particularly business elites, tended to trust neither the central government nor the local governments, instead lending their support to nonprofit organizations as one choice of welfare (Himmelstein 1996). Traditionally, business elites believed that the governments were too inefficient to deliver the various services that were needed, and they disliked the intervention by governments to the private sphere. Therefore, private companies took the initiative and began contributing to a lot of fields in social welfare. (In the first figure in Figure 7.2, corporate philanthropy in the

U.S. society is shown by the black dotted area where civil society intersects with the business sector.)

Over many years, the U.S. government has seen that nonprofit organizations can deliver efficient services. By the late 1970s, nonprofit organizations became a major provider of social welfare services, and the government became a major financial provider (Salamon 1999). Salamon calls such cooperation between the government and nonprofit organizations as "the third party government."

The features of civil society, such as voluntary contribution and autonomy, are more remarkable in the United States than in Japan. For instance, the amount of contribution by each household in Japan is JP¥3,000 per year, which is 1/60 of the amount those in the United States give (Asahi Shimbun, June 18, 2005). Like Japan, nonprofit organizations in the United States are supported by the government; however, they maintain more autonomy than those in Japan. This is probably due to where the finance comes from. When we compare sources of finance in the voluntary sector between Japan and the United States, in Japan, 52 percent is from admission fee and service fees, 45 percent is from the government, and only 3 percent comes from philanthropy. In the United States, the figures are 57 percent, 30 percent and 13 percent, respectively (Salamon 1999). Therefore, the nonprofit sector in Japan depends on the government more than that in the United States.

Because many Japanese corporations do not fully understand corporate philanthropy, the business sector of Japan tends to participate less than their U.S. counterparts (In Figure 7.2, it is indicated by the size of the black dotted area between Japanese society and American society). However, we should not ascribe the lack of understanding of civil society to the responsibility of corporations. It arises from a social situation in which citizens and corporations do not expect social contribution, especially in the area of welfare, by enterprises. Because local communities in Japan have little expectation that enterprise will contribute to social welfare, the corporations also do not feel the necessity of it. Both citizens and corporations are not fully aware of what social contribution by enterprise can achieve for the local communities, and in many cases, those communities expect nothing more from business than the sponsorship of town festivals.

Summarizing the discussion so far, it can be concluded that the American government's role in social contribution, particularly in welfare, is much less than its Japanese counterpart. In contrast, corporations in the United States take a more significant role in social contribution than those in Japan, directly or indirectly through nonprofit organizations. The difference arises from the social expectations of corporate philanthropy, which was formed in the process of social development.

NOTES

1. The most recent data shows that the number of NPOs in Japan is close to 40,000 (Asahi Shimbun, June 21, 2009). So, it is steadily increasing in Japan.

2. Recent growth of NPOs in Japan means that the line shaded area has expanded. As Japan enters into the aging society, welfare expense will increase rapidly. The growth of NPOs means a competition between NPOs and public interest corporations. It is expected to bring down the cost in welfare. So, the legislation of the NPO Law is in accordance with a trend toward a smaller government.

3. Recently, the expectation for government's active role in social welfare provision has resurfaced in Japan, as a response to the global economic crisis that started in 2008, ignited by the collapse of the subprime mortgage market in the United States. The event shed a light on the negative consequences of former Prime Minister, Junichiro Koizumi's structural reform, which in reality cut the budget for welfare.

4. It should be noted that poverty has become one of the major social issues for Japan in the last few years. In 2000, there was a nationwide debate over whether the middle class in Japan had collapsed or not (Chuo Koron 2001). Now, however, the debate has shifted to poverty. For example, *Ronza*, a popular Japanese journal, featured poverty in its January 2007 issue (Ronza 2007). In October 2008, *Hinkon Kenkyu* (Poverty Research), a semiannual journal specializing in poverty (mainly in Japan), was published by Akashi Publishing Company. Various statistics indicate the growing instances of poverty in Japan. The number of non-regular employees, the number of households that receive public assistance, and the number of people whose income is less than 2 million yen (approximately US$20,000) has increased over the last ten years. Also, the relative poverty rate in Japan is 13.5 percent—that designates Japan as having the second highest rate of poverty incidence among all OECD countries (Asahi Shimbun, April 30 2008). Japan's long praised reputation as an egalitarian society is the thing of the past. Therefore, right now, the safety net instituted by the government is outdated and not working well.

5. The massive layoffs of temporary workers since December 2008, due to the world economic crisis, have made people reconsider the idea of smaller government which was ambitiously promoted by Koizumi administration.

Chapter Eight

Learning about Corporate Giving

INTRODUCTION

As described in the previous chapters, corporate giving was developed in the United States. In contrast, Japan does not historically have a tradition of corporate giving, and only recently have Japanese businesses begun to engage in more corporate giving, especially in the areas of education, arts and culture, in Japan.[1] Japan has been experiencing a changing normative expectation of corporate giving, although it is not practiced at a grass-roots level, as it is in the U.S. For Japanese in America, the encounter with corporate philanthropy began when they opened offices and factories in the United States, and as with other American customs, corporate philanthropy was a foreign concept to Japanese corporations, who considered paying taxes and providing stable jobs as their main corporate citizenship role (Bob and SRI International, 1990). Japanese companies began to appear in the United States during the 1950s, the first of which to arrive were trading companies that opened offices to sell Japanese products within the U.S. Large manufacturing companies soon followed, first opening sales offices and then building factories. These pioneering Japanese companies did not have any knowledge in dealing with cultural differences or experience in the American way of business practice, and labor relations and labor practices have since become a major issue for most Japanese companies in the U.S. For example, in the United States, the typical relationship between management and the union has been one of conflict, while in contrast, the relationship between management and the union in Japanese companies is usually cooperative. Hence, Japanese companies did not know how to deal with this conflict. The diversity of American society was also problematic for Japanese corporations, who had little experience of the labor practices related to minority issues. The result was discriminatory hiring on behalf of the company, and law suits soon followed. In another example of labor practices, a company offered company cars to Japanese expatriates, which in Japanese common sense, is taken for granted and no one thinks of it as a problem. However, this became an issue with American employees, who later sued the company. Another issue that became a point of struggle was the different wage levels between Japanese and American employees.

These struggles experienced by the pioneering Japanese corporations convinced them it was important to observe American culture and customs in order to survive in the United States. It also began the ground work for what would become Japanese corporate philanthropic activities in later years. However, it wouldn't be until the late 1980s that Japanese corporations felt they could divert any attention away for their core business activities to those of a philanthropic nature. When they did, it was largely in response to the shifting political climate between Japan and the United States. Before the mid-1970s, Japanese manufacturing companies exported products to the United States, such as automobiles and consumer electronics, while having restrictions against the import of products from overseas, especially agricultural products, in an effort to protect domestic producers. This unfair practice resulted in a huge trade deficit for the United States and a trade surplus for Japan. In the late 1970s, when the deficit became too large, the United States announced a Voluntary Restraint Agreement, in which the Japanese government implemented a self-imposed trade restriction on exported Japanese color televisions. In 1981, this self-imposed restriction was extended to the export of Japanese automobiles. At the same time, Japanese manufacturing companies experienced the appreciation of the yen. The Plaza Agreement of 1985 drastically changed the exchange rate of the yen against the US dollar, with the yen appreciating so much that it was almost impossible for some Japanese export companies to make a profit.

These events left Japanese companies with no other rational choice than to directly invest in the United States, and by 1988, this investment reached more than US $50 billion, up from US $5 billion in 1980 (Bureau of Economic Analysis in Bob and SRI International, 1990). However, while it was welcomed in many of the communities that had lost their American factories to Mexico and the South, at the national level and in other communities, Japanese direct investment was perceived as a threat to America. The Japanese companies began buying large amounts of real estate, including part of the Rockefeller Center, and to many Americans, carried the symbolic meaning that the Japanese would conquer America through money. A survey by Bob and SRI International (1990) shows a similar climate to this time. In answering a question: "overall, how do you feel about Japanese direct investment in the United States?," 28.1 percent of the respondents answered "strongly disapprove," while 23.0 percent said they "somewhat disapprove." Thus, more than half of the respondents had a negative feeling about Japanese direct investment. In addition, 84.3 percent of the respondents agreed to the question that "Japan is America's greatest economic competitor." This study suggests that this political environment necessitated Japanese companies to look towards corporate philanthropy as a strategic way to ease these tensions. The early years of law suits also taught them to follow the American ways of business practice. In this context, Japanese corporations have learned about corporate philanthropy as a process of adaptation to American culture, and in the process, Japanese companies must determine whether they are:

a) An "American" company that happens to be Japanese owned; or
b) A "Japanese" company that happens to be operating in the U.S.

Their answer to this question determines their corporate identity, and might influence the nature and level of corporate philanthropy.

LEARNING FROM LITERATURES

Literature has been an important resource for Japanese corporations to learn about corporate philanthropy in the United States. Daily Japanese newspapers and magazines specializing in economy and international trade often write about the business climate in the United States, as well as corporate giving in America. Since Japan does not have many activities associated with corporate giving, simply to write about it is newsworthy. Furthermore, as described in chapter 7, the coverage of corporate philanthropy in America was natural for the Japanese media, because the social expectation for civil society was spreading in Japan.

Companies usually subscribe to these magazines and newspapers, requiring employees at a management level to look through these materials regularly as a part of their duties. Therefore, Japanese employees in the Japanese companies of Heartland were found to be quite knowledgeable on the issue of corporate giving. The manager of Dainichi said:

Well, many things about America like this [corporate philanthropy] come from magazines and readings that deal with the management of Japanese companies overseas. When we read Japanese newspapers, this issue is also discussed. Well, if we are interested in society in general, we can see the trend and mechanisms of society [through readings].

In response to the question, "Where did you learn about the business roles of a wider community?" a GTS manager replied. "It is from literature. We learned it from literature, such as newspapers, and what they say in those readings. When we read those periodicals, there were often those articles related to corporate philanthropy."

Primarily, Japanese expatriates have been required to read many articles on corporate philanthropy in America. By the time they are transferred to the U. S. operations, expatriates are knowledgeable about these issues, and they have a basic understanding of what's going on in America. The fact that Japanese expatriates are knowledgeable about corporate giving is mentioned by Martin Walsh of the United Way of America, whose job was to build relationships between the United Way and foreign-owned companies. He says that:

> *There were a few times when United Way encountered difficulty in recruiting foreign-owned companies [and] we felt that this was a result of foreign executives not understanding what we were about. The companies were almost always small to medium-sized businesses, often operating in large anonymous industrial parks. Typically, they would be led by a British or German executive who just didn't understand the concept of federated giving, and resisted involvement in principle. However, we could bring some of them around over time. Interestingly enough, Japanese executives would know about United Way: their company or trade association would have briefed them. Their reservations and questions were much more related to what other companies were giving in the local community rather than United Way's operating principles (Conference Board, 1994).*

This comment also shows a Japanese tendency toward the normative aspect of philanthropy, as discussed in previous chapters.

The powerful Japanese business association, the Keidanren, is the force behind this understanding. The Keidanren (Japan Federation of Economic Organizations) was established in 1946, and consists of 121 industrial organizations and 1,009 leading companies. The mission of the Keidanren is to resolve domestic and external problems in the business community, as well the promotion of healthy economic development (Council for Better Corporate Citizenship, 1998). It also has a strong relationship with the ruling Liberal Democratic Party and bureaucrats. In contrast to the United States, the Japanese government and the private sector have a more symbiotic relationship, and by working together towards national economic development goals, they help each other to forge the shape the Japanese economy.

Sensing that Japanese direct investment was not welcomed in the United States, the Keidanren started to think about ways to ease these tensions. Realizing that corporate citizenship was a role that Japanese corporations could play, this was seen as a good strategy for easing these tensions and gaining acceptance in American communities. For these reasons, the Keidanren established the Council for Better Investment in the United States (CBIUS) in April, 1988. This council was replaced by the Council for Better Corporate Citizenship (CBCC) in September, 1989, which encourages Japanese affiliated companies to become good corporate citizens in their host communities. Member companies learn about corporate citizenship in the United States through seminars, lectures and forums. The council also publishes around 3,000 copies of their newsletter "Stakeholders," which is distributed to CBCC members and other Japanese affiliated firms located in the United States. This newsletter has valuable information about community relations, such as what other companies are doing, and gives examples of how to implement community projects. The CBCC also dispatches a mission once a year for meeting with Japanese affiliates, American firms, state officials, business organizations and others, to discuss community needs or community relations activities. The council has led Japanese companies in the United States toward a better understanding of what corporate citizenship means in America. In addition to the Keidanren, other business associations, such as the Doyukai, have also established committees on corporate citizenship (Taka, 1997).

Japanese companies already within the United States also learn about corporate philanthropy from literature, and many of the larger Japanese corporations have established foundations and contributions departments in their American headquarters. For example, Kagoshima has a contributions department headed by an American director in its headquarters in New Jersey, and has also created an independent foundation in the United States. The primary role of these foundations and contributions departments is to send out corporate giving information to branch offices and factories. Thus, Japanese management in Japanese affiliated corporations has developed sufficient knowledge about what corporate philanthropy is in America. A GTS manager said: "It [corporate giving in America] did not surprise me, because I have already had an imprinting [through reading literature] about corporate giving in America. Because I have imprinting, it is natural to think that we should do something for philanthropy."

Literature provides Japanese employees with a basic understanding of the corporate giving culture in the United States, through which they learn the importance of having a good relationship with the community, and what is expected of them in terms of corporate activities within that community. The establishment of foundations and corporate giving departments by large Japanese companies is a starting point for this understanding. Even though they do not understand corporate philanthropy comprehensively, they have at least established a framework.

LEARNING FROM AMERICAN EMPLOYEES

Although literature on corporate philanthropy enables Japanese employees to reach a basic level of understanding, they do not necessarily grasp the full concept, and still need to internalize it as a part of their business function. This process of internalization cannot be achieved through literature alone: it needs to be a process of interaction between Japanese and American employees, in order for Japanese firms to understand the nuances of corporate philanthropy. American employees are the most valuable source of information, and are the ones who really carry out these philanthropic activities for the Japanese companies in Heartland.

Because Kagoshima and GTS were originally founded in the U.S. through the acquisition of American companies, they have been in a better position to learn the ways of American corporate philanthropy than their other Japanese corporate counterpart, Dainichi. Whirlpool Corporation built a plant in 1971 to produce vacuum cleaners, employing over eleven hundred workers. When the company announced its decision to move out of Heartland, the Industrial Foundation took the initiative to sell and transfer the plant, and in August, 1990, Kagoshima bought 75 percent of the shares, while Whirlpool retained 25 percent. This new company, which was renamed Kagoshima Floor Care Company, produced Kenmore brand vacuum cleaners for Sears. In October 1994, Kagoshima purchased the remaining shares (25 percent) from Whirlpool, renaming the company again to Kagoshima Appliance Corporation. In the process of the sale and transfer, 80 percent of the employees and managers were retained by Kagoshima, and although this was a logical decision on Kagoshima's behalf, due to the production of similar products and, therefore, the adoption of Whirlpool's production system, the plant does not have a Japanese flavor. The same is also true for corporate philanthropic activities. Non-profit organizations kept sending letters soliciting donations from Kagoshima, thinking that only their name had changed from Whirlpool to Kagoshima. This was done without any concern for the changes that would impact on the level of company contributions. On the part of the recipients, they had a similar level of expectation of contributions from Kagoshima, and therefore, approached the company in the same way they had Whirlpool.

The basic attitude of Japanese management towards the opinions or suggestions of American managers and employees regarding corporate philanthropy is to follow them as closely as possible. A Kagoshima manager says:

> *Basically, these philanthropic activities have, after all, close adherence to the community. That's why I think these activities are a part of business that Japanese expatriates cannot make decisions [about]. It is not like these management styles that have a common ground [between Japanese and American]. It differs*

from community to community. Well, basically, I think it is best to respect the opinions of the local [American employees]. They have lived in this community for decades. We Japanese expatriates, who have been here just for half a year, cannot judge and make decisions. That's why, basically, most of the time, we respect local [American employees'] opinions.

As a multinational corporation, Kagoshima has many facilities around the world, especially in Asia and North America. This experience has allowed them to develop the philosophy that a good business can be possible only when they develop a cooperative relationship with the local community. Based on this, the company has adopted five mottos for Japanese employees who are transferred to the United States: First, "Do it for yourself," which asks Japanese employees to actively challenge themselves in everything, without fear of mistakes. Second, "Work together," that is, Japanese employees need to know and understand America and work together with Americans. Third, "Be a good citizen," is said to be achieved through bringing "individuality" and "freedom" into one's own life, by participating in community activities. Fourth, "Make one person like you," which means to mentor an American who works like you. Fifth, "Truly realize what 'being Japanese' means," suggesting that Japanese employees try to understand the differences between Japanese and Americans, and what to do from there. These philosophies and mottos reflect the importance of the community and the American people, and attempt to motivate Japanese employees to respect the suggestions and opinions of their American counterparts. In Kagoshima, when there are solicitations for donations, the Japanese managers go to the top American management and ask for their opinions, asking how such a case was handled in the past. In addition to this, the suggestions of American employees are also considered, only after which, they compare these with Kagoshima's company philosophy. If these solicitations contradict the company philosophy, they will be dropped from the consideration process. Thus, it can be said that American employees and managers have a strong influence on the final decisions of the selection process.

GTS also started with an existing American company, which was initially a Firestone operation. In spring 1970, Firestone engineers opened a pilot operation, and due to its success, it became a full-fledged steel-cord producing operation in 1974. In 1981, Yokohama Rope Manufacturing Company Ltd., in conjunction with Itochu and Mitsubishi, purchased the Firestone operation, renaming it GTS Wire & Cable Co., Inc. The production has grown considerably, adding to its customer base major tire companies such as Goodyear, General Tire and Dunlop.

GTS's core philosophy of overseas operation is localization, that is, respecting local customs. Although the degree of localization is not as deep as other Japanese companies that came to the United States in the 1950s, GTS's parent company, Yokohama Rope Manufacturing Company, understands the importance of respecting local customs. A GTS manager says that: "[in regards to monetary contributions], headquarters in Japan thinks it is unavoidable to spend money. We got permission from Japan to do that. Anyway, we say 'don't make your community your enemy.' We must think that way." At GTS, an American has been assigned to the general manager's position, in which the decision making for contributions is a part of his duties, and the policies for corporate giving are determined by this person. The Japanese management does not intervene with policy making: Instead, their role is to allocate the annual budget for contributions, without saying anything about how or to whom the money should be donated. As an American, the general manager understands the expectations of the local community in regards to corporate giving, as well as how many non-profit organizations there are, what they do, who they are, and their credibility. By delegating the job to an American, GTS has managed to be a member of the Heartland community.

Unlike Kagoshima and GTS, Dainichi began its operation as a brand new, 100 percent Japanese owned enterprise in 1995, and although it is still to reach the maturity level of Kagoshima or GTS, it has been trying to establish itself as a sound business operation ever since. From its inception, the company had to establish hiring policies, wage levels and fringe benefits, and initiate policies on corporate philanthropy. Most of the employees were line workers, and there were few Americans working in the office. Those that did were not extensively experienced in management, especially in the area of public relations. The only exception was an American plant manager, who had been promoted to the position from the Lexington-based Clark Company. Although he did not have specific knowledge about corporate giving, he understood where to get information from, and had connections with community leaders; thus, he was given the responsibility for corporate philanthropy, giving his opinions to the Japanese management regarding which solicitations the company should take. He also winnows the important solicitations from those that are not. Since there is no explicit corporate giving policy, he is pushing management to devise one, so that, in the case of unsuccessful solicitations, reasons can be provided to non-profit organizations and employees. At Dainichi, he is still learning how to best handle the issues related to corporate giving, without much assistance from the other American employees. While a defined corporate giving policy still needs to be established, other employees are only suggesting activities in which they want to participate, such as the March of Dimes and Big Brothers & Big Sisters. Meanwhile, Dainichi needs more time to establish corporate giving as a part of their business strategy.

LEARNING FROM THE COMMUNITY

The city of Heartland is a vibrant community, where social capital has long been nurtured, and the Japanese companies in the city are well integrated into a social network of industrial community leaders. These Japanese corporations are benefiting through this social network, with the Industrial Council being their most important connection to the community. This Council is utilized not only by Japanese companies but also by American companies for information and advice. At a monthly meeting, the presidents and plant managers of Heartland's manufacturers discuss the issues affecting their business, in which corporate philanthropy is also an issue being discussed. Usually, practical questions are raised, such as, when a non-profit organization visits a company, the company will go to the council and ask what kind of a non-profit organization it is, and whether it is worth donating to or not. Its members feel that, although the council is not necessarily close knit, there has been enough trust established between them to allow delicate information to be shared, and thus created a field in which they can interact freely.

Dainichi, as a new company with no established policies on philanthropy, has had to rely on this network for much needed information. A manager said: "when we first started talking about corporate giving, I questioned GTS officials about how did you do it, how did you decide what campaign would you get involved in. Also, questioned B. B. Fishwater, not just the Japanese owned company." For a newcomer like Dainichi, who is eager to learn about business practices in Heartland, it is only reasonable to learn from other, well established corporate neighbors, who have successful businesses in the community. It makes sense to do what they have already done successfully, and not waste time doing things different, which could lead to costly mistakes. This cooperative way of information sharing creates a pattern of corporate giving; because they shared information about the nature of non-profit organizations in Heartland and the surrounding area, company choices for donations tend to be similar. Therefore, many manufacturing companies in Heartland donate a large portion of allocated philanthropic money to the United Way, along with two or three other major organizations, such as the March of Dimes and the American Red Cross, and small amounts to other agencies.

Direct contact with non-profit organizations is another way Japanese corporations learn about the expectations placed on corporate philanthropy in the United States. Unlike Japan, there are many people and agencies in the United States who casually and frequently knock on the front door of companies, soliciting donations or support. These include organizations such as fire departments, brass bands, schools, retired groups (such as the police), welfare agencies, youth groups, and senior citizens' groups, among many others. Every one of the Japanese corporations in Heartland has experienced this type of encounter, and through this, has learned a great deal about what kind of expectation the community has. How they respond to these expectations is determined through consultation with their employees and industrial neighbors.

There is a major difference between Kagoshima and Dainichi, in terms of where they source their information on corporate giving. Kagoshima retained more than 80 percent of the American employees from Whirlpool, including many management level staff members. Having had experiences in dealing with corporate giving, they know about non-profit organizations in the community, and often the person who approaches the company. As such, it is not critical for Kagoshima to rely on the Industrial Council for information on corporate giving, and in fact, Kagoshima's attendance at the monthly meetings is lower than that of Dainichi or GTS. On the other hand, Dainichi does not have any employees who are familiar with corporate giving, coupled with the fact that they are too new to know about the nature of all the non-profit organizations within the area. The plant manager himself does not have enough knowledge about corporate giving and agencies in Heartland, and therefore the community, and especially the Industrial Council, has become key sources of information. Since Dainichi's plant manager is eager to contact other neighboring industries for information and advice, it is only natural that Dainichi's attendance at the council meeting is significant.

COMPARISON OF AMERICAN AND JAPANESE COMPANIES ON CORPORATE GIVING

As previously discussed, how Japanese view philanthropy differs greatly from most Americans. This is partly due to the fact that most Japanese view social services, such as those for the homeless, the handicapped or the poor, as being the responsibility of the government (London, 1991). Instead, Japanese people view philanthropy as the donation of money for arts and culture. However, since the economic slump of the 1990s, Japan has seen a sharp increase in the number of homeless people living near train stations or in the parks of larger cities. In such a historically egalitarian society, such visual signs of poverty are a relatively new phenomenon, bringing it closer to the reality found within the United States.

On the contrary, poverty and homelessness are a day to day affair in the United States, and taking care of affected people is relegated, at least in part, to the private sector. The work of non-profit organizations and private welfare agencies has become indispensable to the society, and American citizens expect these agencies to take care of the less unfortunate, having little trust in the government to be responsible for this task. This mindset stems from a historical legacy that stretches back to the formation of America. In the early days of settlement, communities were created in which people took care of themselves. Since government functions usually came into the community later, the mentality of 'taking care of our own' still survives (Bob and SRI International, 1990). Business elites have distrusted the government, and view corporate philanthropy as a form of protection from encroachment by the government into the private sector (Himmelstein, 1990). In addition, citizens fear that if the task is handed down to the government, it will cost many times more than private agencies. The government also understands the importance of the private sector and thus, has created legislation to facilitate such private sector activities. An example is the 1986 U.S. Tax Code, Section 501(c) (3), which encourages individuals and organizations to donate money towards philanthropic activities. As discussed thus far, in the United States, philanthropy is associated with social welfare, and people imagine social welfare when they think about philanthropy, and organizations such as Salvation Army; in Japan, on the other hand, philanthropy is associated with culture and education. As discussed in the previous chapter, these different views on corporate giving are embedded in the divergent ideas of civil society between the U.S. and Japan.

Though still not as widespread as in the United States, many major Japanese companies in Japan now have formal functions or offices that deal with corporate philanthropy, and their names are an indication as to what kind of philosophy they subscribe to, and the type of tasks they do. They often include the heavy use of the words "culture" or "environment." Examples include: the public relations department, the social contribution office, the office of environmental and cultural promotion, the office of cultural promotion, the social and cultural office, public relations' social & cultural office, the office of global environment, public relations' social welfare department, and the office of social contribution promotion.

Kagoshima's headquarters in Japan has a social and cultural department which deals with corporate philanthropy. The department mainly focuses on culture, volunteer work and education; the majority of their activities are in the area of culture. For example, they promote music events, classical music concerts, traditional Japanese dance concerts, choirs and plays. Volunteer work is not so much related to welfare work, as in the United States, but it is about planting trees and promoting the work of JICA (Japan International Cooperation Agency), an equivalent of Peace Corps in America. Education is mainly targeted towards nature preservation or nature appreciation activities. For example, they conduct seminars for those who are interested in becoming a guide for observing nature. It is also a common request for people to research their neighborhoods and find out how much natural preservation exists; this is especially true for rivers. Social welfare activities, such as donating food and blankets for the homeless and offering financial help to families in emergency situations, are common in the United States, but in Japan, as Kagoshima's social and cultural department shows, it is quite different. Kagoshima's corporate giving does not include these types of social welfare activities for Japanese citizens; instead, they have social welfare activities for people in developing countries. Basically, Japanese corporations do not feel a need to engage in social welfare activities, because such activities are regarded as being taken care of by the government.

Aside from large corporations like Kagoshima, many Japanese companies do not fully understand what corporate philanthropy is all about. As mentioned in the previous chapter, this lack of understanding comes from a social condition where citizens, corporations and communities do not have a high expectation of corporate giving related to welfare. Kagoshima, one of the leading companies in corporate citizenship in Japan, is aware of this lack of consciousness relating to philanthropy in local communities, and they feel a need to promote corporate citizenship in local plants and branch offices. A manager said:

> *As our corporate standing, we establish a so called 'social cultural department' in the organization, so that we can actively engage in corporate philanthropy, because if our headquarters does not establish it and do it, then our local branches will not participate in it. Our branches are located in communities throughout Japan. Each local branch is busy doing their daily business activities. They do not have time to look at and participate in social contribution. Therefore, we established a social and cultural department at our headquarters so that it can set an example for local branches, and set a policy for corporate philanthropy.*

The difference between the American and Japanese conceptions of philanthropy makes it difficult for Japanese workers in the United States to understand corporate giving in America; therefore, they try to learn as much as they can through literature, fellow employees and the community. As they have a different conception of philanthropy, it seems that Japanese workers in America take it on face value, and they engage in corporate philanthropy because they feel it helps them to assimilate into American society, and therefore find success in business. Therefore, in their real mind, they think they have no choice but to do it. A Kagoshima manager said that:

> *I feel like Japanese corporations do philanthropy because they are lured by American companies. I doubt that Japanese corporations understand the inner*

meaning of corporate philanthropy. I think, I feel like, because surrounding corporations do (corporate giving), American corporations do, I, we, too, have to do that.

Well, I feel Japanese corporations end up with only the methodology of mecenat [support and protection of art and cultural activities]. I doubt that these activities really contribute to social contribution. Well, I feel something these activities end up with at the level of surface because we just do mecenat activities, and volunteer activities only when they are given.

Many Japanese managers feel the same way as this Kagoshima manager. As Japanese, they are still in the process of learning the essential meaning of philanthropy in America.

Corporations, particularly, American companies that understand the meaning of corporate citizenship, are very active in local communities because they understand that corporate philanthropy is part of their business responsibility in society, and needs to be a part of their overall business strategy. In other words, American corporations understand it is beneficial for their business. As such, they have embraced the idea that corporate giving is social welfare that benefits not only the local citizens, but also their own employees who live in the community. They also understand that being involved in community activities helps improve employees' morale and increases their productivity. By doing so, it creates a good corporate image that helps to increase sales. Although small to medium sized Japanese corporations have yet to make these connections, large Japanese corporations have just begun to. In sum, most Japanese companies are still in the process of learning about the nature of social responsibility in America.

NOTE

1. Although corporate philanthropy is a relatively new concept to the Japanese, philanthropy by religious groups (in this case, Buddhism) has existed since the eighth century. The first modern Japanese foundation, the Society of Gratitude, was founded in 1829 (Hustedde, 1997).

Chapter Nine

Conclusion

SUMMARY OF FINDINGS

Company Philosophy

Recruiting and retaining a good workforce has been an important factor for business success in recent years. Many corporations have realized this fact, and some have developed the mindset that corporate philanthropy is a good strategy to recruit and retain the best workers, believing this active participation makes them more attractive to potential employees.

This research shows that an understanding of the relationship between corporate giving and the recruitment & retention of workers is determined by the national origin for the ownership of the company. That is, American companies, such as Goodman and B. B. Fishwater, understand this relationship well, and act accordingly by being active in community improvement activities. On the other hand, British company Fortson does not share this philosophy, believing instead that a corporation has no need to be involved in community activities, and should not spend its shareholders' investments in such a way. For Japanese companies, the understanding of the relationship between corporate philanthropy and recruitment & retention of workers depends on the duration of the company's presence in the United States. For example, Kagoshima established its first American office in 1959, and seems to understand the relationship, acting accordingly. Meanwhile other companies, such as GTS and Dainichi, do not fully understand this relationship, both having the philosophy that a company's responsibility is for its shareholders and employees only. Instead of seeing the connection between corporate giving and the recruitment & retention of employees, Dainichi sees a conflict between them. Although GTS does not fully perceive the relationship, they do modestly contribute to the community. This is because GTS has been in Heartland for 20 years and understands the community expectations that corporations should be involved in community giving.

It is interesting to note that in addition to the company's philosophy, the CEO's personal philosophy can also shape the behavior of corporate philanthropy. Fortson's president is a good example of this. Being an American, he understands the community's expectations, as well as the relationship between corporate giving and the recruitment & retention of its workers. Motivated by enlightened self-interest and altruism, he has developed a corporate culture that facilitates corporate philanthropy, even though the parent company does not support such activities.

Firm Size and Corporate Giving

In sociology, size has been studied as a factor for influencing organizational structure and behavior. In this research, firm size was examined as an independent variable in describing the organizational characteristics and behaviors of corporate philanthropy. Specifically, this study looked at whether there is a relationship between the size, nature, and level of corporate giving.

Useem (1988) showed that larger companies give more money to charitable causes than smaller companies, reasoning that because larger companies tend to have formalized corporate philanthropy, they can allocate money, regardless of profits. This research partially supports this argument in relation to Japanese companies. For example, Dainichi, the smallest company, does not have a contribution department in either Heartland or Japan, and its corporate donations are dealt with by managers on case by case basis. Therefore, the company has no formalized way of allocating money for community activities. GTS, a medium sized company, like Dainichi, does not have a contributions department, and its corporate donations are being handled by an American manager without any corporate policy on philanthropy. On the other hand, Kagoshima, the largest company, has corporate giving departments in both its Japanese and the U.S. headquarters, as well as an established foundation for philanthropic activities. However, in the Heartland plant, there is no such department; instead donation money is handled by a panel of managers whose decision is influenced by the contribution department in the U.S. headquarters. For example, they will only allow the United Way to come into the company for a fund raising drive, which is a policy made by the contribution department in the U.S. headquarters. In sum, the largest Japanese company in this study has a formalized contribution system in place at its headquarters, and thus, it partially supports Useem's formalization argument.

Mixed results have been indicated in the relationship between size and the level of corporate social responsibility. McEloy and Siegfried (1984) found that the relationship is non linear, that is, medium sized companies contributed the most to charities, while large and small companies contribute less. In contrast, Mitchell (1989) found a positive relationship; as a company becomes larger, it is likely to contribute more toward charity. In focusing on Japanese companies, Lombardo (1991) claims that size and the length of time in the United States influences the degree of participation in corporate philanthropy. This research found that the largest Japanese company contributes the most, while medium sized and small companies contribute less. The largest, Kagoshima donated US $81,802.54 to the United Way in 1999. This was $51.13 per employee. GTS's contribution to the United Way was $26,087.03, and Dainichi's donation was $1,996.40. In terms of per employee, both companies have similar amount, $39.29 for GTS and $39.15 for Dainichi. This finding is similar to Lombardo's finding.

As for American companies, the findings of this research indicate that there is no clear relationship between firm size and the level of corporate giving. When comparing the ranking of donation amounts given to the United Way, as well as the ranking of the number of employees, it is difficult to discern any patterns. This finding is in line with a study by the Conference Board (1994), which showed no association between firm size and corporate giving. The presence of the association for Japanese companies and non-presence of the association for American companies are also indicated in the interviews for this study. In contrast to Japanese corporations, which often mentioned size as a contributing factor for philanthropy, American corporations gave no indication that size was a factor in their decisions relating to corporate giving.

In comparing American and Japanese companies, American companies are more generous philanthropic contributors, with their employees pledging US $114.44 per person, while their Japanese counterparts only contributed $47.42 per employee.

An interesting finding revealed that Heartland's retail chain stores do not contribute much to the community, which is in sharp contrast to the manufacturing companies, which believe that contributing to the community is also an investment in their workers.

Learning about Corporate Giving

In recent years, and largely due to American influence, Japanese society and corporations have embraced the idea of corporate philanthropy. However, the idea of corporate philanthropy as it developed in the United States is foreign to Japanese. Therefore, the philosophy and practices of corporate philanthropy in Japan are different from those of the United States. In Japan, the main focus of corporate philanthropy is in the area of culture, environment and education, whereas American companies focus on social welfare. For example, the social and cultural department of Kagoshima in Japan spends most of its budget on cultural events. Due to this difference in conception, Japanese corporations in the United States must learn about the American way of corporate philanthropy. This study revealed the three main avenues that Japanese corporations rely upon for gaining such an understanding: through literature related to corporate philanthropy, by learning from their fellow American employees, and by learning what the expectation of the community are in relation to corporate giving.

Before transferring to U.S. factories, Japanese managers begin reading Japanese newspapers and business magazines, which usually report on business issues in the United States, including reports on corporate citizenship. Through this literature, they gain a general knowledge of corporate philanthropy in America. Japanese business associations also disseminate information on corporate citizenship to their member companies through periodicals, lectures, and seminars.

When operating in America, Japanese corporations learn about corporate giving through practicing it, and their American employees are an important asset for this. GTS and Kagoshima bought their operations from American companies. They began their operations as joint ventures with American companies, and retained their American employees, who knew how to conduct corporate philanthropy. Kagoshima, in particular, kept more than 80 percent of its employees, including managers from the previous American operation, and they in turn have taught the concept of corporate citizenship to the Japanese managers. Dainichi is at a disadvantage in terms of gaining knowledge on corporate philanthropy from its employees, because the company started its operation from scratch. It simply does not have managers and employees who are knowledgeable about corporate giving, and as a result, its American manager turns to the community for more information.

The same community has been a vital resource for Japanese companies. Those that operate in Heartland receive solicitations for donations from many individuals and non-profit organizations, and through these encounters, Japanese firms learn more about the expectations of the community when it comes to corporate philanthropy. In addition, meetings of the Industrial Council are important occasions where Japanese corporations can gain valuable information from other firms regarding non-profit organizations such as what they do and whether or not a contribution is worthwhile. This network of Heartland

businesses helps Japanese corporations learn about the local American expectations of business practices.

IMPLICATIONS

One of the purposes of this study is to clarify the current state of philanthropic
activity undertaken by Japanese manufacturing companies in America. This
is an important task in the applied sociology, which aims to use sociological
knowledge for the betterment of society and the community. Observations
within this research contain some suggestions for non-profit organizations
that seek donations, as well as Japanese corporations that have a desire to be
more active in corporate philanthropy.

Ostrander and Schervish's discussion (1990) on donor-oriented strategies
is helpful when trying to understand Dainichi's contribution behavior. In
exchange philanthropy, a type of donor-oriented strategy, a company donates
money because friends of executives asked them to and the company hopes
for some return in the future. Each year, Heartland has a Great American
Brass Band Festival, for which they always ask for corporate sponsorship.
Until 1999, Dainichi had not sponsored this event, but gave US $1,000 in
that year—a significant amount of money for the company at the time. The
sponsorship was not the result of any interest in the Festival per se, but because they were asked by other Japanese companies to participate, and because a Japanese high school brass band was participating. Due to influential
Japanese expatriates in the area wanting 100 percent participation by local
Japanese companies, they asked Dainichi to join the cause. It is possible that,
had the other Japanese companies not asked, Dainichi would not have been a
sponsor. Japanese companies have the tendency to watch what other companies do and act accordingly. Therefore, it is more effective for non-profit organizations to solicit donations from all Japanese companies in the area. Once
they get one company to accept, it is a good strategy to ask to the company
to invite other Japanese companies. As the realm of civil society is expanding
in Japan since the enforcement of the NPO Law in 1998, it is more likely to
encounter Japanese managers and workers who have some understanding of
the participation in social welfare by citizens and corporations.

Another suggestion for non-profit organization is to target American managers when soliciting donations. Since Japanese society does not place the
same importance on community and corporate philanthropy as Americans
do, Japanese managers rely on American employees, especially management
level Americans, for information and decision-making on such matters. Japanese managers know the principle of corporate giving philosophy; however,

they do not understand the many practical aspects of such giving. By convincing American managers about a cause, non-profit organizations can more effectively solicit donations from Japanese companies. Also, it is important for non-profit organizations to provide information about the potential benefits of active corporate philanthropy to the business. Corporations that are active in philanthropy identified the relationship between corporate giving and the benefits received by their businesses. According to business and community leaders, active participation in corporate philanthropy helps to improve the community in which employees live. When employees see the company's corporate citizenship role improving their quality of life and community, they tend to become satisfied with and proud of the company. As a result, they are motivated to work harder for the company and more likely to stay with the company longer, which in itself is a great reward for the company. Many Japanese companies do not perceive this connection, and tend to think of corporate philanthropy as an extra activity that takes money and resources away from core business activities. Making this connection between corporate giving and the benefits received by participating businesses will help to bring in more donations and volunteer work from Japanese companies.

This research also has suggestions for Japanese companies. Since it is necessary to participate in corporate giving, regardless of the amount given, Japanese companies should utilize corporate giving as part of their business strategy. This can not only enhance the image of both the company and its products, but also tends to increase employee satisfaction. Japanese companies tend not to announce their contributions to the community, but by publicizing their commitments to the community, they will obtain a better reputation, and with it, quality workers and an improved retention rate (Greening and Turban, 2000). Japanese companies should also realize the benefits beyond productivity, as calculated by output divided by hours worked in employee volunteerism. Japanese companies are usually reluctant to make such calculations believing instead that the use of work hours for volunteerism reduces productivity. If productivity is only viewed in terms of the output divided by hours worked, it can be considered as wasting money. However, if we look at the employees' morale level and subsequent productivity, it far outweighs the productivity derived from the mere simple calculation. Employee volunteerism is a very effective way of improving general employee morale and satisfaction.

LIMITATIONS OF STUDY

It is important here to remember that, as a case study, the results of this research cannot be used as a generalization applied to all American, British or Japanese firms operating in the U.S. Furthermore, Heartland itself may be a somewhat unique community compared to others in America, given the prominent role that the Industrial Council plays in the life of the community.

SUGGESTIONS FOR FUTURE RESEARCH

The purpose of this study was to explore the relatively new phenomenon of corporate social responsibility in Japanese manufacturing firms that are located in the U.S. It was hoped that this study would identify the problems pertinent to sociological or broader social science theories and concepts. The discussions below are some observations and findings that may refine sociological and social science theories, and help to compare these with previous research findings.

Aupperle's (1982) discussion on the hierarchy of organizational needs helps to understand the difference between Kagoshima and Dainichi on corporate giving behaviors. Borrowing the idea from Maslow, Aupperle argued that Carroll's (1982) concept that the four dimensions (economic, legal, ethical and philanthropic) of corporate social responsibility can be understood as a macro motivation of society. The dimension was arranged from a lower level to a higher level, based on the needs of the organization, with the lowest need being economic, followed by legal, ethical and philanthropic needs. It was not reasonable to meet the higher level needs before that of the lower level are met.

Dainichi sees economic performance, that is, generation of profit for shareholders, and employee's wages and benefits as the most important things to consider. They also believe that philanthropy is not a critical part of their business strategy. As a recently established company, Dainichi tries to meet the lower need of the organization first, that is, its economic dimension. On the other hand, Kagoshima, a long standing company in the United States, has already met the basic needs of economic, legal and ethical dimensions. Now, it is the philanthropic dimension of its organizational needs they are working on. It appears that this hierarchy of needs is more applicable to Japanese corporations, especially new comers to the United States. In contrast, the American companies seem to have narrowed the gap between the philanthropic dimension and the need of the other dimensions. For example, Goodman has spent a lot of money on philanthropy, even though they had been in the red. The same is true for other American companies. Thus, in America, the philanthropic dimension has moved to a lower hierarchy of organizational needs. Therefore, Aupperle's concept of the hierarchy of organizational needs should be reconceptualized.

This research was qualitative, and it has merit with the topic of corporate citizenship. As discussed in Chapter 2, Pinkston and Carroll (1994) compared American companies with those from England, France, Germany, Japan, Sweden and Switzerland on corporate social responsibility issues. They looked at corporate citizenship issues, finding no statistical difference among those companies from different countries. There are two items of corporate citizenship issues that are of interest here: contributions to philanthropy, and employee volunteerism. Pinkston and Carroll's research indicated that Japanese corporations and American corporations have no difference on corporate philanthropy. However, this research shows that in terms of monetary contribution, American manufacturing companies are more generous than their Japanese counterparts. For example, Kagoshima's contribution to the United Way was US $51.13 per employee, while GTS Wire & Cable's donation to the United Way was $39.29 per person. On the other hand, B. B. Fishwater's contribution to the United Way was $104.32 per employee, and on average, each employee at Blue Wing Shoe Company donated $160.76.

In terms of attitudes or views toward corporate citizenship, American corporations are more willing to commit than Japanese corporations. A director of the United Way mentioned that Japanese companies are reluctant to release their employees to the Day of Caring activities. In comparison, American companies tended to have a deeper understanding of the benefits employee volunteerism has, by seeing that it improves their morale and, eventually, their productivity. Since the results are varied and not much qualitative research has been done in this area, it is desirable to study this issue through qualitative methods, such as those used in this study.

Institutional theories in organizational research are found to be useful in understanding the corporate behaviors of Japanese manufacturing companies on corporate philanthropy. Well institutionalized among American manufacturing companies, there is no discussion on whether or not philanthropic donations are worthwhile for business strategies. However, Japanese manufacturing companies are not yet convinced that corporate philanthropy is beneficial for their businesses. Thus, the degree of institutionalization of corporate social responsibility is less for Japanese than American companies. Among the Japanese companies, Kagoshima has institutionalized corporate social responsibility more than Dainichi or GTS. This is because Kagoshima is a large corporation, having a longer presence in the U.S. The higher degree of institutionalization related to corporate social responsibility among American manufacturing companies is due to an influence from the cognitive and normative structures of institutions. American corporations understand the relationship between corporate social responsibility and its benefits to their businesses. Therefore, they are willing to participate in it, which is in the realm of the cognitive structure of the institution. In the case of Japanese corporations, the influence of the cognitive structure of the institution is less evident, due to their lack of understanding of the relationship between corporate giving and the benefits it may have to their businesses.

The normative structure of an institution is operated in both American and Japanese corporations. Community expectations of corporate philanthropy for the manufacturing companies in Heartland encourage these companies to become involved in community improvement activities. Kagoshima feels more pressure from the community than Dainichi, and due to its size, feels a greater responsibility for the welfare of the community. In future research, it would be interesting to see the degree of institutionalization by quantifying the normative and cognitive structures of institutions by comparing them in various dimensions (e.g., by country of origin, by community, and by firm size).

This research has shown that the Industrial Council is an important network in the Heartland community. It can be perceived as an embodiment of social capital that encourages coordinated actions for community development. The Industrial Council has encouraged its corporate members to be active in community improvement activities. Does the existence of social capital in the community make difference to the behavior of Japanese manufacturing companies? In the future, comparison with other communities is needed to answer this question.

Another research topic for consideration is: Once a company decides to engage in corporate giving, what factors influence the areas of giving? In other words, do companies prefer one area over another (e.g., social welfare, arts/culture, education, environment, recreation)? Are there cultural differences in the preferences? Given the fact that corporate philanthropy in Japan focuses on arts/culture, environment and education more than social welfare, these questions can clarify the nature of corporate giving further.

In summary, this study examined the concept of corporate social responsibility in Japanese manufacturing companies in Kentucky. The concept of corporate social responsibility illuminates the intersection of business and community/society. In addition to offering jobs and paying taxes, corporate philanthropy becomes a tool for corporations to be involved in communities. Japanese corporations in America try to understand these functions of corporate philanthropy by interacting with both their American employees, and the communities they are in.

Appendix

Table A1. List of Japanese Companies in Kentucky (2002)

Community	Company Name	Year Est.	Emp.	Location of Parent Company
Ashland	AK Steel Corp.	1989	1,400	Tokyo
Bardstown	FET Engineering, Inc.	1988	30	Aichi
	AMB Inc.	1995	47	Kanagawa
	American Fuji Seal Inc.	1968	400	Osaka
	Johnan America Inc.	1998	10	Nagano
	Inoac Packaging Group	1988	200	Aichi
	Jideco of Bardstown, Inc.	1986	500	Kanagawa
	Trim Masters, Inc.	1991	311	Aichi
	Intertec Systems LLC	1987	159	Aichi
Berea	Kentucky Steel Center	1996	26	Tokyo
	Matsushita Electric Motor Corp. of America	1995	115	Osaka
	KI (USA), Inc.	1988	300	Kanagawa
	Tokiko (USA), Inc.	1987	760	Kanagawa
Beaver Dam	Daisel Safety Systems America, LLC	2001	24	Osaka
Bowling Green	TWN Fastener, Inc.	1988	75	Osaka
	NASCO	1986	234	Kanagawa
	Bando Mfg. of America	1988	156	Tokyo
	Kiriu USA Co. Ltd.	2001	30	Tochigi
	Sumitomo Electric Wiring Systems	1993	78	Osaka
	Waltex	2002	35	Tokyo
Calvert City	ICT Inc.	1992	35	Osaka
Campbellsburg	Arvin Sangyo, Inc	2002	64	Aichi
Campbellsville	Murakami Manufacturing USA	2001	30	Shizuoka
Edmonton	Sumitomo Electric Wiring System	1988	693	Osaka

(*continued*)

127

Table A1. (*continued*)

Community	Company Name	Year Est.	Emp.	Location of Parent Company
Elizabethtown	Cytech Products, Inc.	1988	14	Aichi
	AP Technoglass Corp.	1988	589	Tokyo
	Ambrake Corporation	1987	1005	Tokyo
Erlanger	Obara Corporation	1988	56	Kanagawa
	Toyota Motor Manufacturing North America Inc.	1996	790	Aichi
Flemingsburg	Toyo Seat	1997	266	Hiroshima
Florence	IT Spring Wire	1997	50	Tokyo
	Aristech Acrylics LLC	1990	298	Tokyo
	International Mold Steel Inc.	1993	20	Aichi
	Tenryu America Inc.	2000	5	Shizuoka
	Mazak Corporation	1968	558	Aichi
Frankfort	Indiana Die Tec Inc.	2002	12	Aichi
	Mishima Tech America Inc	1997	14	Fukuoka
	Topy Corporation	1986	504	Tokyo
	Ohi Automobile America Corp.	1990	350	Kanagawa
Franklin	Franklin Precision Ind.	1990	370	Aichi
	New Mather Metals	2001	NA	Kanagawa
	Toyo Automotive Parts	2001	25	Osaka
Georgetown	AT & O Tech	2001	10	Aichi
	ECO Technology	NA	NA	Aichi
	Kentucky Advanced Forge LLC	2001	2	Aichi
	Trinity Industrial Corp.	1987	68	Tokyo
	Vuteq Corporation	1987	178	Aichi
	International Crankshaft	1990	140	Tokyo
	Toyota Tsusho America Inc.	1986	350	Aichi
	Louisville Forge & Gear Works LLC	1985	310	Aichi
	Toyota Motor Mfg. USA	1987	7600	Aichi
Glasgow	ACK Controls, Inc.	1989	297	Tokyo
	AMAK Brake LLC	1994	462	Tokyo
Harrodsburg	Trim Masters, Inc.	1988	147	Aichi
	Trim Masters, Inc.	1988	585	Aichi
	Hitachi Automotive Products (USA) Inc.	1985	893	Tokyo
Heartland	Dainichi Manufacturing Corp.	1994	40	Tokyo
	GTS Wire & Cable	1981	591	Tokyo
	Kagoshima Appliance Corp.	1990	1000	Osaka
Hebron	Toyota North America Parts Center Kentucky	2000	324	Aichi
Hopkinsville	Amfine Chemical	1999	35	Tokyo
	Freudenberg Nonwovens Ltd.	1973	238	Tokyo
	Sun Chemical Corp	1998	43	Tokyo
	TG Automotives Sealing Kentucky	2002	65	Aichi
	Douglas Autotech Corp.	1994	196	Shizuoka

Community	Company Name	Year Est.	Emp.	Location of Parent Company
	Meritor Suspension Systems Co.	1992	160	Tokyo
	CoPAr, Inc.	1988	196	Tokyo
Lawrenceburg	YKK Universal Fasteners, Inc.	1987	300	Tokyo
	Four Roses Distillery LLC	1946	42	Tokyo
Lebanon	Curtis-Maruyasu America	1998	375	Aichi
	TG Kentucky LLC	1999	457	Aichi
	NSU Corp	2001	8	Aichi
Leitchfield	Trim Masters, Inc.	1997	424	Aichi
Lexington	Toyo Lex Industry Corp	1998	7	Aichi
	Accuromm USA, Inc.	1989	36	Aichi
	Link-Belt Const. Equipment	1986	665	Tokyo
	Kito USA	1999	19	Tokyo
London	Aisin Automotive Casting LLC	1996	480	Aichi
Louisville	Nova Steel Processing Inc.	1996	20	Tokyo
	Yamamoto FB Engineering	1995	73	Saitama
	Bioproducts	1981	22	Tokyo
	Ameristeel	1968	37	Osaka
	Riverport Steel, Inc.	1989	62	Tokyo
	Miyama USA, Inc.	1991	68	Shizuoka
	Wako Electronics (USA) Inc.	1988	140	Osaka
	Zeon Chemicals, Inc.	1989	400	Tokyo
Maysville	Mitsubishi Electric Automotive	1995	242	Tokyo
	Green Tokai Co. Ltd.	1996	220	Aichi
	Techmotrim Inc.	1987	290	Tokyo
Munfordville	Akebono Corporation	1995	47	Tokyo
Nicholasville	Trim Masters, Inc.	1993	202	Aichi
Owensboro	Toyotetsu Mid America LLC	NA	NA	NA
Paris	Central Manufacturing Co.	1989	490	Aichi
Park City	JASCO International	2002	10	Tokyo
Richmond	Kokoku Rubber, Inc.	1988	150	Tokyo
	Richmond Auto Parts Technology	1998	149	Aichi
	Enersys Inc.	1991	472	Osaka
	AFG Industries Inc.	1998	242	Tokyo
	Nichidai America Corporation	NA	NA	Kyoto
Russell Spring	Hitachi Cable	NA	NA	Tokyo
Russellville	JS Technos Corporation	1989	75	Tokyo
Scottsville	Sumitomo Electric Wiring Sys.	1987	280	Osaka
	Sumitomo Electric Wiring Sys.	1988	185	Osaka
Shelvyville	Katayama America Co.	1989	320	Okayama
	Alcoa Fujikura, Ltd.	1985	50	Tokyo
	Ichikoh Mfg., Inc.	1987	260	Tokyo
Somerset	Toyotetsu America Inc.	1995	507	Aichi
Sonora	NSU Corporation	1997	60	Aichi
Springfield	Springfield Products, Inc.	1990	275	Aichi
	Akebono Corporation	2002	14	Saitama *(continued)*

Table A1. (*continued*)

Community	Company Name	Year Est.	Emp.	Location of Parent Company
	Parker SDS	1977	225	Kanagawa
	Toyotomi-America Co.	1999	100	Aichi
Stanford	Lincoln Manufacturing Inc.	1995	55	Kanagawa
Versailles	YH America, Inc.	1989	406	Tokyo
	United L-N Glass, Inc.	1987	450	Tokyo
Walton	Waltex	1994	25	Tokyo
	Clarion Corp. Of America	1987	75	Tokyo
	Dynamec Inc	1992	200	Shizuoka
Williamsburg	Firestone Ind. Products	1989	350	Tokyo
Winchester	Nova Steel Processing Inc.	1986	8	Tokyo
	Advanced Green Components LLC	1997	55	Hyogo
	Ainak Industries Co. Ltd.	1997	79	Aichi
	Wintech, Inc.	1995	340	Ibaraki
	Fuji Univance Corporation	1996	100	Shizuoka
	Kagoshima Appliance Corp.	1995	85	Osaka
	Ohi America Corporation	1994	260	Kanagawa

(Kentucky Cabinet for Economic Development, 2002)
Notes:
Total number of Japanese firms in Kentucky = 126
Total number of employment in Japanese firms = 35,556
Heartland's figures are from 2002. Thus, the numbers are different from those in the text.

References

Abe, Kinya. 1995. *Seken to wa Nanika* (What is Seken?). Tokyo: Kodansha. (Japanese).

Abrams, Dominic, Kaori Ando and Steve Hinkle. 1998. "Psychological Attachment to the Group: Cross-Cultural Differences in Organizational Identification and Subjective Norms as Predictors of Workers' Turnover Intentions." *Personality and Social Psychology Bulletin* Vol.24 No.10, October, 1027–1039.

Akiyoshi, Mito. 2006. "The Constitution of Social Capital and Support Systems: A U.S.-Japan Comparison" A paper presented at the annual meeting of the American Sociological Association, Montreal Convention Center, Montreal, Quebec, Canada, August 11.

Amenomori, Takyoshi and Tadashi Yamamoto. 1998."Introduction" in *The Nonprofit Sector in Japan*. Edited by Tadashi Yamamoto. Manchester: Manchester University Press, pp. 1–17.

Asahi Shimbun (Asahi Newspaper). 2005. *"NPO Houjin 2 Man Dantai Toppa* (NPO Organizations Exceeded 20,000)." February 16, Morning Edition. (Japanese).

———. 2005. *"Kifu Bunnka: Zeisei no Ato oshi de Hagukumo* (Contribution Culture: Let's Nurture It by the Support of Tax System.)" July 18, Morning Edition. (Japanese).

———. 2008. *"Henten Keizai-Shogende tadoru Dojidaishi: NPO Houan-Gin ritsupo wo mezaso* (Transition Economy, Contemporary History Traced by Testimony: NPO Law, Let's Aim at Legislation by House Members.)" Februrary 9, Morning Edition. (Japanese).

———. 2008. *"Reporutaajyu Nippon* (Reportage Nippon)." April 30, Morning Edition. (Japanese).

———. 2009. *"Kawaru Hatarakikatai: Saiteichingin Kurasenai* (The Changing Working Style: We Cannot Live by the Minimum Wage.)" June 7, Morning Edition. (Japanese).

———. 2009. *"Kohin Syakai: Sasaeai wo Motomete* (A Society of the Poor Public Provision: Searcing for Mutual Support)." June 21, Morning Edition. (Japanese).

Asahi Shimbun Company. 2007. "*Gendai no Hinkon* (Poverty Today)" *Ronza.* January 2007. (Japanese).

Aupperle, I. E. 1982. *An Empirical Inquiry into the Social Responsibilities as Defined by Corporations: An Examination of Various Models and Relationships.* Doctoral Dissertation, University of Georgia.

Beechler, Schon and John Zhuang Yang. 1994. "The Transfer of Japanese-style Management to American Subsidiaries: Contingencies, Constraints, and Competence." *Journal of International Business Studies*, Fall, v25 n3 p467.

Benedict, Ruth. 1946, 2006. *The Chrysanthemum and the Sword: Patterns of Japanese Culture.* Mariner Books.

Berle, A. A. and Gardiner C. Means. 1932. *The Modern Corporation and Private Property.* New York: Macmillan.

Berman, Melissa A. 1994. *The Future of Workplace Giving.* #1073-94-CR. Conference Board.

Besser, Terry L. 1998. "The Significance of Community to Business Social Responsibility." *Rural Sociology,* 63(3), 412–431.

Blau, Peter M. and Richard A. Schoeuherr. 1971. *The Structure of Organizations.* New York: Basic Books.

Bob, Daniel E. and SRI International. 1990. *Japanese Companies in American Communities: Corporation, Conflict and the Role of Corporate Citizenship.* New York: Japan Society.

Brammer, Stephen and Andrew Millington. 2004. "Stakeholder Pressure, Organizational Size, and the Allocation of Departmental Responsibility for the Management of Corporate Charitable Giving." *Business & Society.* Vol. 43. No.3. September.

Brilliant, Eleanor L. 1990. *The United Way.* New York: Columbia University Press.

Brown, C. and J. Medoff. 1989. "The Employer Size-Wage Effect." *Journal of Political Economy.* 97, 1027–59.

Brown, Richard C. 1992. *A History of Danville and Boyle County Kentucky 1774–1992: An Official Project of The Kentucky Bicentennial Celebration.* Danville, KY: Bicentennial Books.

Burlingame, Dwight F. and Patricia A. Frishkoff. 1996. "How Does Firm Size Affect Corporate Philanthropy?" In *Corporate Philanthropy at the Crossroad.* Edited by Dwight F. Burlingame and Dennis R. Young.

Carroll, Archie B. 1998. "The Four Faces of Corporate Citizenship." *Business and Society Review,* Winter.

Charmaz, Kathy. 1983. "The Grounded Theory Method: An Explication and Interpretation." In *Contemporary Field Research: A Collection of Readings.* Edited by R. M. Emerson. Boston: Little Brown.

Chuo Koron Editorial Department, ed. 2001. "*Ronso: Cyuryu Houkai* (Debate: Collapse of the Middle Class.)" Tokyo: Chuo Koron Shinsha. (Japanese).

Chronicle of Philanthropy. 1994. "The Midwest's Charitable Advantage." February, 22, 1, 22–26.

Coleman, James S. 1988. "Social Capital in the Creation of Human Capital." *American Journal of Sociology.* 94, September.

Council for Better Corporate Citizenship. 1998. A Brochure.

Dacin, M. Tina. 1997. A Book Review for Institutions and Organizations by W. Richard Scott. *Administrative Science Quarterly,* December, 821–824.

Davis, Keith. 1973. "The Case for and against Business Assumption of Social Responsibilities." *Academy of Management Journal*, 16(2):312–322.

Deming, W. E. 1986. *Out of the Crisis.* Cambridge, Mass: Massachusetts Institute of Technology, Center for Advanced Engineering Study.

Diamond Big Company. 2001. *"Daigakusei Syusyoku Ninnkido Ranking"* (A Ranking of Popular Companies among College Students.) (Japanese).

DiMaggio, Paul J. and Walter W. Powell. 1991. "The Iron Cage Revisited: Institutional Isomorphism and Collective Rationality in Organization Fields." In *The New Institutionalism in Organizational Analysis.* Edited by Walter W. Powell and Paul J. DiMaggio. Chicago: The University of Chicago Press.

Eberly, Don E. 2000."The Meaning, Origins, and Applications of Civil Society" Chapter 1 in Eberly Don E. (ed.)_The Essential Civil Society Reader: The Classic Essays in the American Civil Society Debate.* Lanham, Maryland: Rowman & Littefield Publishers, Inc., pp. 3–29.

Ebrahimpour, Maling. 1988. "An Empirical Study of American and Japanese Approaches to Quality Management in the United States." *International Journal of Quality and Reliability Management.* 5, pp5–24.

Ebrahimpour, Maling and John B. Cullen, 1993. "Quality Management in Japanese and American Firms Operating in the United States: A Comparative Study of Styles and Motivational Beliefs," *Management International Review*, February v33 n2 p23.

Economic Planning Agency, The Government of Japan. 2000. *White Paper on the National Lifestyle: Volunteering Enriches Societies with Taste-linked Human Relations.*

Friedman, Milton. 1971. "Does Business Have a Social Responsibility?" *Bank Administration.* April, 13–14.

Galaskiewicz, Joseph. 1991. "Making Corporate Actors Accountable: Institution Building in Minneapolis-St. Paul." In *The New Institutionalism in Organizational Analysis.* Edited by Walter W. Powell and Paul J. DiMaggio. Chicago: University of Chicago Press.

Galper, Joshua. 1999. "An Exploration of Social Capital, Giving and Volunteering at the United States County Level." Working Paper.

Greening, Daniel W. and Daniel B. Turban. 2000. "Corporate Social Performance as a Competitive Advantage in Attracting a Quality Workforce." *Business & Society,* Vol.39 No.3, September, 254–280.

Hall, Peter Dobkin. 1982. *The Organization of American Culture, 1700–1900: Private Institutions, Elites, and the Origin of American Nationality.* New York: New York University Press.

Hamashima, Akira, Takeuchi Ikuro and Ishikawa Akihiro eds. 2005. *Shakaigaku sho Jiten* (The Compact Dictionary of Sociology), new and enlarged edition. Tokyo: Yohikaku. (Japanese).

Harada, Masazumi. 1999. "Minamata Disease and the Mercury Pollution of the Globe." Environmental Information Network for Asia and the Pacific.

Hartley, Jean F. 1994. "Case Studies in Organizational Research." In *Qualitative Methods in Organizational Research: A Practical Guide*. Edited by Catherine Cassell and Gillian Symon. London: SAGE Publications.

Hasegawa, Koichi, Chika Shinohara and Jeffrey P. Broadbent. 2007. "The Effects of 'Social Expectation' on the Development of Civil Society in Japan." *Journal of Civil Society,* Vol. 3, No. 2, 179–203.

Hay, Robert and Ed Gray. 1974. "Social Responsibilities of Business Managers." *Academy of Management Journal,* 17, 135–143.

Hendry, Joy. 1995. *Understanding Japanese Society, Second Edition.* New York, NY: Routledge.

Himmelstein, Jerome L. 1996. "Corporate Philanthropy and Business Power." in *Corporate Philanthropy at the Crossroads*. Edited by Dwight Burlingame and Dennis R. Young. Bloomington: Indiana University Press.

Hodgkinson, Virginia Ann et al. 1997. Giving and Volunteering in the United States. Washington, DC: Independent Sector.

Hougland, James G. 2001. "Public Perception of Toyota Motor Corporation in Kentucky." In *Japan in the Bluegrass*. Edited by P. P. Karan. Lexington, KY: University Press of Kentucky.

Hustedde, Ronald J. 1997. "American Nonprofit Organizations and Community Development." *Journal of Korean International Society of Community Development.* Vol.7, December, 95–109.

Japan External Trade Organization (JETRO). 1991. *1991 JETRO White Paper on Foreign Direct Investment.* Tokyo, Japan.

Jemison, David B. 2001. *Study of Community Involvement in the Austin Area by Established and Entrepreneurial Firms.* Austin, TX: The McCombs School of Business, The University of Texas.

Jepperson, Ronald L. 1991. "Institutions, Institutional Effects, and Institutionalism." in *The New Institutionalism in Organizational Analysis*. Edited by Walter W. Powell and Paul J. DiMaggio. Chicago, IL: The University of Chicago Press.

Japan External Trade Organization (JETRO). 2008a. *"Nihon no Kuni Ciki betsu Taigai Chokusetsu Toshi Zandaka* (Japan's Outward Direct Investment by Country and Region)". *Boeki, Toshi, Kokusai Syushi Tokei* (Japanese Trade and Investment Statistics). Tokyo, Japan. (Japanese).

Japan External Trade Organization (JETRO). 2008b. *"Boeki Aitekoku Rankingu* (Ranking of Trade Partner)". *Boeki, Toshi, Kokusai Syushi Tokei* (Japanese Trade and Investment Statistics). Tokyo, Japan. (Japanese).

Jones, Marc T. 1996. "The Poverty of Corporate Social Responsibility." *Quarterly Journal of Ideology*, 19(1–2):57–72.

Karan, P. P. 2001. *Japan in the Bluegrass.* Lexington, KY: University Press of Kentucky.

Karan, P.P. and W.A. Bladen. 2001. "Japanese Investment in Kentucky." In *Japan in the Bluegrass*. Edited by P.P. Karan. University Press of Kentucky. Pp.15–41.

Kentucky Cabinet for Economic Development. 2004. *Announced/Reported Japanese Investment in Kentucky.* Frankfort: KY.

———. 1999. *Announced/Reported Japanese Investment in Kentucky.* Frankfort: KY.

Kentucky Post. 1995 December 5, 1996 March 14, 1996 November 12.

Klier, Thomas H. and Kenneth M. Johnson. 2000. "Effect of Auto Plant Openings on Net Migration in the Auto Corridor, 1980–97." *Economic Perspectives.* v24, i4, pp.14–29.

Kono, Toyohiro and Stewart Clegg. 2001. *Trends in Japanese Management: Continuing Strengths, Current Problems and Changing Priorities.* New York: Global Publishing at St. Martin's Press.

Leedy, Paul. 1997. *Practical Research: Planning and Design.* NJ: Prentice-Hall, Inc.

Lexington Herald Reader. 1995, December 10, 1996 March 7.

Lofland, John and Lyn H. Lofland. 1995. *Analyzing Social Setting: A Guide to Qualitative Observation and Analysis.* New York, NY: Wardsworth Publishing Company.

Logan, David. 1994. *Community Involvement of Foreign-Owned Companies.* No. 1089-94-RR. New York: Conference Board.

Lombardo, Barbara J. 1991. "Japanese Corporate Philanthropy in the United States." *Nonprofit Management & Leadership,* Vol.2 No.1, Fall.

London, Nancy R. 1991.*Japanese corporate Philanthropy.* New York: Oxford University Press.

Lynn, Leonard H. 2002. "Trends in Japanese Management: Continuing Strengths, Current Problems and Changing Priorities, (Book Review)." *Pacific Affairs,* Summer, v75 i2 p291(2).

Market and Opinion Research International. 2000. *SMEs' Attitudes to Social Responsibility.* London: Business in the Community.

Marx, Jerry D. 1998. "Corporate Strategic Philanthropy: Implications for Social Work." *Social Work.* Vol. 43. No. 1. pp. 34–41.

McElroy, K. M. And J. J. Siegfried. 1985. "The Effect of Firm Size and Mergers on Corporate Philanthropy." in *The Impact of the Modern Corporation.* Edited by Betty Bock, Harvey J. Goldschmid, Ira M. Millstein, and F. M. Scherer. New York: Columbia University Press.

Meyer, J and B. Rowan. 1977. "Institutionalized Organizations: Formal Structure as Myth and Ceremony." *American Journal of Sociology.* Vol. 83. pp. 340–363.

Miller, Paul and Charles Mulvey. 1996. "Unions, firm size and wages." *Economic Record.* June v72 n217 p138.

Mitchell, Neil J. 1989. *The Generous Corporation: A Political Analysis of Economic Power.* Connecticut: Yale University Press.

Mroczkowski, Tomasz and Masao Hanaoka. 1998. "The End of Japanese Management: How Soon?" *Human Resource Planning,* Sept, v21 i3 p20.

Nakane, Chie. 1970. *Japanese Society.* Berkeley, CA: University of California Press.

Nelson, R. 1970. *Economic Factors in the Growth of Corporate Giving.* New York: National Bureau of Economic Research.

Nippon Hoso Kyokai (NHK). 2008. *NHK Supesharu: Kinkyu Repoto – Shakai Hosyo ga Abunai* (NHK Special: An Immediate Report - Social Security is in Danger). A TV program broadcasted on May 11.

Nosco, Peter. 2002.Confucian Perspectives on Civil Society and Government" in *Civil Society and Government.* Edited by Rosenblum, Nancy L. and Robert C. Post. Princeton, NJ: Princeton University Press. Pp.334–359.

Ostrander M. and Schervish L. 1990. "Philanthropy as Social Relations." In *Critical Issues in American Philanthropy. Strengthening Theory and Practice.* Edited by Jon Van Till and associates. San Francisco, CA: Jossey-Bass.

Perrucci, Robert. 1994. "Embedded Corporatism: Auto Transplants, the Local State and Community Politics in the Midwest Corridor." *The Sociological Quarterly.* Vol. 35, Number 3, pp.487–505.

Pfeffer, Jeffrey. 1983. "Organizational Demography."In *Research in Organizational Behavior, vol. 5,* edited by L.L. Cummings and Barry M. Staw. Greenwich, Conn.: JAI Press.

Pfeffer, Jeffrey and Gerald R. Salancik. 1978. *The External Control of Organizations.* New York: Harper & Row.

Pinkston, Tammie S. 1994. "Corporate Citizenship Perspectives and Foreign Direct Investment in the U.S." *Journal of Business Ethics,* 13, 157–169.

Pinkston, Tammie S. and Archie B. Carroll. 1996. "A Retrospective Examination of CSR Orientations: Have They Changed?" *Journal of Business Ethics 15,* 199–206.

Post, James E. 1996. "The New Social Contract." in *Is the Good Corporation Dead? Social Responsibility in a Global Economy.* Edited by John W. Houck and Oliver F. Williams. Lanham, MD: Rowman & Littlefield Publication.

Pucik, Vladimir & Nina Hatvany. 1983. "Management Practices in Japan and Their Impact on Business Strategy," In R. Lamb, editor, *Advances in Strategic Management,* Vol. 1, 103–32. Greenwich, Conn.: JAI Press.

Putnam, Robert D. 1993. *Making Democracy Work: Civic Traditions in Modern Italy.* Princeton, NJ: Princeton University Press.

Rosenblum, Nancy L. and Robert C. Post. Eds. 2002. *Civil Society and Government.* Princeton, NJ: Princeton University Press.

Reischauer, Edwin O. and Marius B. Jansen. 1995. *The Japanese Today: Change and Continuity*, Enlarged Edition. Cambridge, Massachusetts: The Belknap Press of Harvard University Press.

Research Institute of Economy, Trade and Industry. 2005. *2005 Nen NPO Hojin Ankeito Cyosa Setuka Hokoku* (A Report on Questionnaire Survey Result about NPO Corporations in 2005). Tokyo. (Japanese).

Rural Culture Association. 2007. "Datsu Kakusa Shakai (Escaping Differential Society)" *Gendai Nogyo* (Modern Agriculture). March issue, Tokyo. (Japanese).

Salamon, Lester M., Helmut K. Anheier, Regina List, Stefan Toepler, S. Wojciech Sokolowski, and Associates. 1999. *Global Civil Society: Dimensions of the Nonprofit Sector.* The John Hopkins Center for Civil Society Studies. Baltimore, MD.

Scott, W. Richard. 1992. *Organizations: Rational, Natural, and Open Systems.* Englewood Cliffs, NJ: Prentice Hall.

———. 1995. *Institutions and Organizations.* Thousand Oaks, CA: SAGE Publications.

Stake, Robert E. 1998."Case Studies." In *Strategies of Qualitative Inquiry.* Edited by Norman K. Denzin and Yvonna S. Lincoln. Thousand Oaks, CA: SAGE Publications.

Tajfel, H. 1978. *Differentiation between Social Groups.* London: Academic Press.

Taka, Iwao. 1997. "Business Ethics in Japan." *Journal of Business Ethics,* 16:1499-1508.

Tillman, Audris D. 1999. *Corporate Contributions in 1997.* #1229-99-RR. Conference Board.

United Way of America. 2000. Leaderboard Summary 1990–2000.

U.S. Department of Commerce, Bureau of the Census. Census 1990.

———. Census 2000.

———. Statistical Abstract of the United States, 1998.

Useem, Michael. 1988. "Market and Institutional Factors in Corporate Contributions." *California Management Review,* Winter, 77–88.

Wendt, Alexander. 1994. "Collective Identity Formation and the International State." *American Political Science Review,* June v88 n2 p384(13).

Wilkinson, Kenneth P. 1991. *The Community in Rural America.* New York: Greenwood Press.

Wolch, Jennifer R. 1995."Corporate Philanthropy, Urban Research, and Public Policy." In *Philanthropy and Economic Development.* Edited by Richard America. Westport, Connecticut, Greenwood Press.

Worthington, Ian, Monder Ram and Trevor Jones. 2003. *Giving Something Back, Social Responsibility and South Asian Businesses in the United Kingdom: An Exploratory Study.* London, UK: Centre For Social Markets.

Wright, Karen. 2001. "Generosity vs. Altruism: Philanthropy and Charity in the United States and United Kingdom." *Voluntas: International Journal of Voluntary and Nonprofit Organizations.* 12 (4): 399–417.

Yanarella, Ernest and Herbert G. Reid. 1990. "Problems of Coalition Building in Japanese Auto Alley: Public Opposition to the Georgetown/Toyota Plant." In *The Politics of Industrial Recruitment: Japanese Automobile Investment and Economic Development in the American States.* Edited by Ernest J. Yanarella and William C. Green. New York: Greenwood Press.

Yang, John Zhuang. 1992. "Organizational and Environmental Impact on the Use of Japanese-style HRM Policies in Japanese Firms in the U.S," *The International Executive.* 4: 321–43.

Yin, Robert K. 1989. *Case Study Research: Design and Methods.* Newbury Park, CA: SAGE Publications, Inc.

Yotsumoto, Yukio. 2001. "Social Impacts of Japanese Businesses in Small Communities of Kentucky." In *Japan in the Bluegrass.* Edited by P.P. Karan. Lexington, KY: University Press of Kentucky.

Index

direct foreign investment, in U.S., 1,
106–7, 108–9
direct observation, 33, 40
documentation, 33
donor-oriented social relations, 13–14

earthquake, Great Hanshin, 94, 95
East Europe, civil society in, 94
Ebrahimpour, Maling, 75n3
economic crisis, global, 104n3, 104n5
economic development, 24
education and training, 24, 37
educational attainment, in Heartland, 48*t*
employee contributions: B. B.
Fishwater, 59, 87, 88*t*, 125; by
group size, 89*t*; company in
Japan *vs.* U.S., 92; Dainichi, 84;
Dancing Corporation, 87, 88*t*;
Fortson Conveyor, 70; Goodman
Incorporated, 87, 88*t*; GTS Wire
& Cable, 84; Huntsman, 87, 88*t*;
Kagoshima, 84; U.S. *vs.* Japanese
company, 120
employees, learning about giving from,
5, 110–12, 121
enlightened self-interest, 10–11
environmental cases: Minamata disease,
25–26, 30n1; Yokkaichi Asthma, 25
environmental responsibilities, of
corporations, 11–12
Erickson McIntosh Regional Medical
Center, 83
exchange philanthropy, 13–14, 122
exploratory study, 32–33

findings, of present study: company
philosophy, 118–19; firm size
and corporate giving, 119–20;
implications of, 122–23; learning
about corporate giving, 120–22;
limitations of, 123–24
Firestone, 111
firm size, 5; American firms in
Kentucky, 87–89; definition of, 38;

formalization of giving relation
with, 78–80, 81–82; level of giving
relation with, 81–86; measures of,
77–78; summary of findings on,
119–20
FKI-PLC, 50, 65
formal contribution department, lack of:
Dainichi, 79–80, 82, 119; GTS Wire
& Cable, 80, 82, 119
formal giving function, reasons for, 79
formalization, definition of, 78
Fortson Conveyer (British parent
company), 42; corporate philosophy
on giving, 64–65; institutionalization
of corporate giving, 90*t*; recruiting/
retention at, 72*t*, 73; understanding/
acceptance of corporate philanthropy,
74*t*
Fortson Conveyer (U.S. president), 45;
CEO personal philosophy, affect on
giving, 68–71, 119; contributions per
employees, 70; corporate philosophy
on giving, 68; recruiting/retention
at, 72*t*, 118, 119; understanding/
acceptance of corporate philanthropy,
74*t*; volunteer work at, 70–71
free rider problem, 17
Friedman, Milton, 18, 64–65, 91
Frishkoff, Patricia A., 79
future research, 124–26

Galaskiewicz, Joseph, 8, 10–11, 14, 15,
17
General County Community
Development Council (GCCDC), 40,
43–44
General County Industrial Council, 46,
47
General County Industrial Foundation,
40, 44–45
generalizations, of present study, 34,
123–24
GHQ, 100
global economic crisis, 104n3, 104n5

Breinigsville, PA USA
03 May 2010
237190BV00001B/4/P